Anna Dervout
@along.avec.anna

Colourwork
in the round

All the techniques you need plus 5 stunning projects

SEARCH PRESS

Introduction

What is colourwork?

Colourwork refers to a knitting technique used to knit patterns with multiple colours. It requires the simultaneous use of several different colours in the same row, an idea that some knitters might find offputting.

Colourwork is used for sweaters, hats, scarves and mittens, but also a wide range of accessories (cushions, Christmas stockings, coasters, and so on). It opens the door to a vast range of knitting motifs: horizontal, vertical, geometric or stand-alone.

Colourwork has been around for many years but has always succeeded in changing with the times. The big, shapeless sweaters of the 1990s have now given way to modern garments with beautiful designs and attractive colours.

The colourwork tradition

The origins of colourwork cannot be attributed to any particular place: colourwork is found in several regions. Fair Isle, Norway, Sweden, Iceland, the Faroe Islands, Estonia, Latvia, Lithuania or the Andes; each country has its own colourwork history.

By way of example, let us take a look at the colourwork of three different regions: Iceland, Fair Isle (one of the Shetland Islands, north of Scotland) and Norway.

Icelandic colourwork

Lopapeysa (the word means 'woollen sweaters') have been an integral part of the country's cultural identity for more than fifty years, but Icelandic colourwork sweaters are, in fact, much older. The wool used, which is very warm and waterproof, was even used by the Vikings to weave the sails of their ships.

The wool from Icelandic sheep is one of the warmest in the world: the long, soft, outer fibres are very tough and water-resistant, while the inner, finer wool, similar to mohair, provides excellent protection against the cold. Originally, *Lopapeysa* were knitted almost exclusively in white, grey, light (or dark) brown and black, which are the natural colours of Icelandic sheep's fleeces. Nowadays, a wide range of colours is available on the market.

Fair Isle

This technique comes from an island off the coast of Scotland, between Orkney and Shetland. The term 'Fair Isle knitting' is now used throughout the world, but this unique style developed on Fair Isle long ago, when the region's knitters discovered that using the stranded knitting technique (carrying the yarn across the back of the work as you go) with fine yarn made it possible to double the thickness of the knit, resulting in warm, but lightweight, garments. Fair Isle generally features a large number of colours (sometimes as many as fifteen or sixteen) and motifs across the garment.

The difference between Icelandic (left) and Fair Isle (right) colourwork.

Norwegian (Scandinavian) colourwork

Norwegian colourwork differs from Fair Isle in that it mainly uses only two colours per project: a main colour and a contrasting colour, generally white contrasting with black, red or blue.

Traditional knitted colourwork motifs differ from country to country but are generally stars, flowers or geometric shapes.

The famous Selbu Mittens are now one of Norway's national symbols. They differ from other mitten designs in that the motifs on the back of the hand and the palm are different and are separated by a vertical line. Another particular feature is that the cuffs on women's gloves are different from those on men's.

Norwegian Mittens for Mimi: pattern by Anna Mazzarella.

Colourwork: who is it for?

Colourwork is suitable for anyone keen to try out a new technique or improve their skills, whether they are novice or advanced knitters. The most important thing is enthusiasm for a new challenge, and the right pattern for your particular skill level.

In this book, we will take a look at the various important steps involved in successfully knitting colourwork in the round. This should give you the confidence you need if you are just starting out, or allow you to choose a more ambitious project if you are already familiar with the technique.

Colourwork and me

For as long as I can remember, I have been fascinated by the Scandinavian countries and their colourwork traditions. Even before I knew how to knit, I dreamt of one day having a hand-knitted colourwork jumper. All the styles looked amazing to me, but I was particularly drawn to Iceland and always wanted to make my very own *Lopapeysa* jumper.

My passion for knitting really began a few years ago while I was pregnant and I became totally hooked on this creative craft. After a few circular knitting projects, I decided to embrace the challenge of colourwork knitting so I could have that famous jumper I had dreamt of, even though the technique appearing a little daunting! A first attempt at a hat was only moderately successful, but undeterred, I decided to launch myself into a sweater with a patterned yoke: this was the Riddari sweater by Védís Jónsdóttir, a traditional Icelandic pattern. I immediately loved this project and after that, I knitted colourwork on a regular basis for my daughter and myself, making up my own designs!

The final part of the book offers you a number of patterns so you can practise the colourwork technique in the round. You have the option to make a child's sweater, a hat, two more sweaters or a woman's cardigan. The garments either use the raglan sleeve technique with a colourwork border or a circular yoke construction with colourwork around the shoulders.

Techniques

CHAPTER 1

The different types of colourwork

The term 'colourwork' covers several different techniques. We will take a look at them one by one so you can get to know how they differ.

In rows or in the round?

You may have heard of, or even tried, colourwork in rows on straight or circular knitting needles. Nowadays, whether you are knitting modern or traditional designs, it is advisable to knit colourwork in the round to make things easier. But what is the difference between colourwork knitted in rows (on straight or circular needles) and colourwork knitted in the round (exclusively on circular needles)?

+ **Colourwork in rows** is a more complicated technique because it requires knitting stitches in different colours on the right side, alternating with the wrong side. This is often a knitter's first attempt, but it is a much more difficult technique to achieve. You need to read the pattern diagram in both directions; that is, all odd rows will be read from right to left and all even rows from left to right. This form of colourwork is not discussed in this book, which focuses exclusively on colourwork in the round.

+ **Colourwork in the round,** a technique that has been used more traditionally, means you only have to knit on the right side of the work. The advantages? First of all, you do not have to knit any rows on the wrong side, so knitting the colourwork is much simpler. The fact that it is simpler means you achieve better tension (gauge), which in turn makes the end result more attractive. The only requirement is that you use circular needles.

Stranded colourwork

Stranded colourwork is the technique generally used in modern or traditional colourwork patterns and is the one that will be used for the patterns in this book.

Adding colours to your knitting is done using the repetition of small designs right across the work. The different coloured yarns used across the row are carried across the back of the work in 'strands', giving the work its name.

Stranded knitting can be roughly divided into two categories, each with its own technique:

+ **Fair Isle,** which follows specific rules, where the designs are generally found over the whole of the sweater or cardigan (body and sleeves); and

+ **colourwork,** which generally refers to all other forms of stranded knitting. It has no defined rules and in some cases is only worked on the yoke, for example.

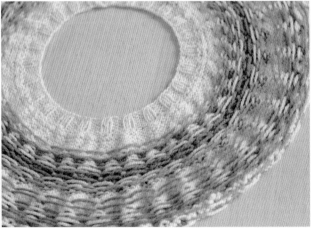

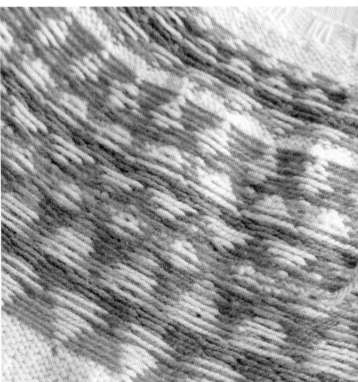

The yarns are knitted or stranded across the back of the work.

Colourwork

I mentioned earlier that stranded colourwork has no particular rules. The majority of modern patterns are therefore colourwork patterns. Traditional colourwork from the Scandinavian countries (Norway, Finland, Sweden) and Icelandic *Lopapeysa* are all classed as colourwork, but not as Fair Isle.

More often than not, the motifs are larger than those of Fair Isle, and can involve more than ten stitches of the same colour in succession. As a result, you need to strand the yarn across the row every seven stitches to maintain good tension. In fact, the only way to get a smooth, even fabric is to have relatively short strands across the back. Stranding your yarn across more than seven stitches without anchoring it can result in a fabric that is uneven, thick and difficult to make look flat and attractive at the blocking stage.

We will look at this in more detail in Chapters 8 and 9 on stranded colourwork and tension.

STRANDING YOUR YARN BEHIND

Stranding the yarn behind requires the colour not being worked to be anchored to the working yarn at regular intervals on the wrong side of the knit, to maintain the tension (gauge) of the whole piece.

Fair Isle

This technique originated in Fair Isle (see page 6). Traditionally, for a pattern to qualify as Fair Isle, it should meet the following criteria:

+ There should be no more than two colours used in the same row: a background colour and a contrasting colour. The grounds for this rule are both practical and aesthetic: it makes knitting easier but also faster. As a result, the tension (gauge) is better and the result neater.

+ In these patterns, you will never find more than seven stitches of the same colour in succession. This ensures that the colour changes occur regularly. They are therefore designed so that there is no need to anchor yarns on the back of the work.

+ The pattern should contain diagonal lines so that the tension (gauge) is evenly distributed. This keeps the work firm but allows it to stretch. In contrast, vertical lines must be used as little as possible as they make the end result somewhat stiff.

+ The patterns used are generally symmetrical and are made up of an odd number of rows. This is not compulsory, but it makes them more attractive and easier to memorize.

+ This type of colourwork is traditionally knitted in the round, using circular needles. Armholes, necklines or front openings (if you are knitting a cardigan) are cut using the steek technique (see Chapter 10, page 88).

+ Fair Isle uses a wool that felts, such as Shetland.

Intarsia colourwork

Intarsia colourwork is another technique used to create one or more motifs across a knit. It is not a stranded colourwork technique but instead uses several balls of the same colour for a single row. It is used, for example, to add a single design in the middle of a knit.

Harry Potter fans might remember the jumpers Mrs Weasley knitted for Ron and Harry, featuring their initials on the front. They used the intarsia technique, rather than stranded colourwork. This type of colourwork is more complicated than stranded knitting, especially for beginners (you will find out why in Chapter 7, page 60).

Right side: the stranded colourwork pattern is repeated right along the row, whereas the intarsia pattern stands alone.

Wrong side: on a stranded knit, the yarn is carried along the whole row, while in intarsia it is not. Several balls of the same colour are used to create the motif.

CHAPTER 2

Materials

As with any knitting technique, colourwork requires the right materials. When it comes to wool, some types of yarn are more suitable than others. It is therefore useful to have a little knowledge on this subject before you begin.

Types of yarn

Traditionally, the yarn used for colourwork, especially Fair Isle, is sheep's wool that has not been chemically treated (non-superwash).

It is interesting to note that, depending on the country and the type of colourwork, different thicknesses of wool are used. For example, Shetland Islands colourwork is usually made from the natural wool of Shetland sheep, which is very fine (4-ply/fingering), giving a swatch size of about 29 stitches per 10cm (4in).

When the colourwork is across the whole knit (Fair Isle), the double thickness of fine wool will ensure the resulting knit is very warm but also lightweight.

Icelandic *Lopapeysa* are often knitted in 100 per cent pure Icelandic sheep's wool, such as the well-known Lettlopí wool (Aran/worsted), which gives a swatch of about 18 stitches per 10cm (4in). When colourwork is mainly confined to the yoke, the sweater is knitted in a thicker, warmer wool.

Animal fibres are the most suitable for colourwork. Before looking at them in more detail, it is important to take a quick look at the difference between two common ways of treating wool you may come across.

Tip

Wool that is not machine-washable is the most suitable for colourwork, especially if you are a beginner. These wools adhere well to your needles and you will find it easier to maintain a good tension (gauge), but what you choose will also depend on what you are making. If you are knitting colourwork socks, you may prefer to use a superwash merino and nylon blend so that the end result is not itchy, washes easily and lasts longer.

+ **Woollen spun yarn** has been carded, spreading out the fibres more loosely, resulting in a woollier, fuzzier fabric. This is the best wool for colourwork, because the stitches will adhere together more easily, resulting in a homogeneous, consistent knit. Example: basic Ulysse or Gilliatt yarns from De Rerum Natura.

+ **Aran (worsted) spun yarn** is repeatedly combed, guiding the fibres in the same direction. This wool will make patterns sharper. It can be used for colourwork but is especially good for knitting cables. Examples: basic Penelope or Albertine yarns from De Rerum Natura (mixed with a little silk).

We will now take a look at the different animal fibres that are used in knitting.

+ **Sheep's wool** (untreated) is the most recommended for colourwork knitting. It is stretchy, but still holds its shape well; it is warm and hard-wearing. There are many breeds: Shetland, Gotland, Bluefaced Leicester, Falkan, Icelandic sheep, and so on.

As wool is generally carded, the fibres, once knitted, do not all lie in the same direction and, as a result, they give a homogenous finish. The wool has the ability to felt slightly, which means the spaces between the stitches are filled. With this type of fibre, the stitches stay in place better and it will be easier to maintain yarn tension (gauge) on the wrong side of the knit.

This type of wool often gives a rustic look, but always check that it is not itchy. This is the case with certain wools, such as Lopí Icelandic wool: it has the reputation of being very rough; however not all rustic wools are itchy. In any case, we all react differently to things, so it is important to test with a swatch.

+ **Merino** comes from a specific breed of sheep and is probably the most common on the market. It is tough but very soft. This wool, which is often Aran (worsted) and can be used for colourwork, does not give the same result as wools such as Shetland. Basically, because it is combed rather than carded, the stitches will not tend to adhere together so much and the patterns will be better defined. However, if you like soft wool, it may be a good choice.

Note that there are also carded merinos (examples include Ulysse and Gilliatt from De Rerum Natura) with a more rustic look, which are then very suitable for colourwork.

+ **Alpaca** is a smooth fibre and drapes nicely. It will not hold its shape as well as sheep's wool, but its main advantage is that it is warmer.

+ **Superwash yarn,** which is machine-washable, is usually merino that has been chemically or electronically treated to destroy its outer layer and prevent the wool from felting in the wash. It is not, therefore, a natural wool, but it is readily available on the market. It can be used for colourwork, but be careful if you are intending to steek (i.e. cut your knitting), as yarns made with this type of wool will not felt and your stitches may unravel at the opening (see Chapter 10 for more details).

+ **Mohair, cashmere and angora yarns** are not recommended for colourwork.

Note that **vegetable and synthetic** yarns, such as linen, cotton, silk and acrylic, are not recommended for colourwork. They are less stretchy and as a result the stitches will be small and the tension (gauge) looser. Cotton, which is relatively heavy and smooth, would give a result that is too thick and uneven. It also has little shape memory and will tend to sag. You will need to wash your knit to restore its shape.

Comparison of superwash merino wool (left) and non-superwash natural sheep's wool (right).

In the sweater on the left, the stitches remain clearly separated and individually defined; in contrast, on the right, they form a unified fabric.

Tip

Choose a type/brand of yarn that offers a wide range of colours, so you have plenty of options in terms of colour combinations.

Tip

To begin with, don't hesitate to practise using thicker wool such as Aran (worsted) for big winter sweaters, or DK (8-ply/light worsted) and 5-ply (sport) for winter and mid-season jumpers. Once you know what you are doing, you could then move on to using 4-ply (fingering). Chunky (bulky) yarns are not recommended for colourwork.

Choosing your yarn

Test out several types of wool and see which suits you best. With time and experience, you will get to know how the different yarns work and can then choose more easily depending on what you want to make and the type of yarn you like to wear.

Initially, you might like to try untreated (non-superwash) wool fibres and, if you are not very keen on the rustic aspect of the wool, opt for merino instead.

In terms of yarn thickness, recommended weights are:

Aran (worsted): a swatch of 18–22 sts for 10cm (4in);

DK (8-ply/light worsted): 20–24 sts;

5-ply (sport): 24–26 sts; and

4-ply (fingering): 26–30 sts.

Chunky (bulky) yarns will be too heavyweight with two strands, while 2-ply (laceweight) will be difficult to knit using several yarns at a time.

Needles

As colourwork is traditionally knitted in the round, circular needles are your go-to choice for this type of project. It is also important to experiment to find out what type of needle (wooden, metal, and so on) suits you best.

Wooden needles (birch or bamboo): these can snag a little at first but quickly polish with use, allowing the stitches to slide smoothly. They are often much loved by knitters.

Metal or carbon needles: these needles are very popular, especially for knitting dry wools, mohair or single wool (textured). They allow the stitches to slide well and they do not damage the wool. Since I discovered metal 'sharp' needles, I have never looked back! They are definitely my top choice.

Plastic needles: these have a little more friction and can make it easier to knit alpaca, silk and cotton. They are recommended for people who knit with a relatively loose tension. Personally, I find they do not allow stitches to slide effectively enough, whatever the type of yarn, so I hardly ever use them.

When knitting small diameters, such as sleeves, mittens or socks, there are several techniques; the equipment you need will differ depending on which technique you choose.

+ If you are knitting using the magic loop technique (see below), you will need a circular needle of at least 60 to 80cm (23½ to 31½in).

+ If you do not use the magic loop technique, you can opt for double-pointed needles, or 23cm (9in) or 30cm (11¾in) circular needles.

THE MAGIC LOOP

This technique allows you to knit small diameters in the round. To do this, the row is knitted in two halves. You work half the stitches while the other half wait on the cable.

Knitting equipment

There are numerous tools and accessories for colourwork knitting; some are essential, some are just very helpful:

+ Ruler or guide for measuring your swatch;

+ Marker rings to help keep track of where you are on the chart, denote decreases/increases and indicate the beginning of a new row;

+ Row counter (optional);

+ Stitch holders;

+ Yarn guides to help you keep your yarns separated while knitting, especially if you are knitting with three yarns at the same time. There are two main types of yarn guides: plastic and metal.

+ Tapestry needle to work in the threads of your knit before or after the blocking stage.

Two yarn guides.

Blocking accessories

Blocking is an essential step in knitting and particularly in colourwork as it allows you to stretch and shape your project to the desired dimensions and give it a more even finish. Here are a few useful items that will help with the blocking process.

+ **Washing detergent for wool:** there are two types of detergents for blocking/washing your knits: washing detergents such as Woolite or Mir Wool, which are the easiest to find (in supermarkets for example), but require rinsing, or more expensive no-rinse detergents (such as Eucalan or Soak). These can usually be found in wool shops or online.

Tip

I usually use a no-rinse detergent when blocking, but I prefer detergents that rinse out when I have worn my garment several times.

+ **Blocking mats:** these are needed so you can stretch out your knit and pin it to dry flat. Real blocking mats are quite expensive, so you can use kids' foam play mats or yoga mats, which will do the job just as well.

+ **Pins and/or blocking combs:** these are used to pin the knitted fabric into its final shape and size.

Tip

After using pins for a long time, I recently bought some blocking combs and I love them! They block clothes well and are easier to use than pins.

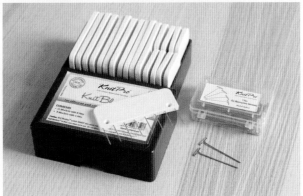

Blocking combs and pins

CHAPTER 3

Reading a colourwork chart

Colourwork design instructions almost exclusively take the form of charts. These make it easy to see how the design will look because the chart will correspond exactly to the pattern you are going to knit.

When looking at a knitting pattern that includes colourwork, don't be intimidated by the charts. In this chapter, we will explain how to tackle this stage.

Reading direction

Charts will be of varying complexity depending on the design you are knitting, but the rules remain the same and are quite straightforward.

+ A chart is always read starting from the bottom-right corner of the chart, always from bottom to top.

  • If the odd numbers are on the right and the even numbers on the left, this indicates that you are knitting in rows. The chart will therefore be read from right to left for odd rows and from left to right for even rows.

  • If the numbers are only on the right, you are knitting in the round. In this case, the chart will always be read from right to left.

+ Each line corresponds to a row and each square corresponds to a stitch.

As you can see, the chart for both methods is the same, but the direction in which you read it and knit it changes depending on whether you are knitting in the round or in rows.

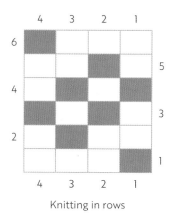

Knitting in rows

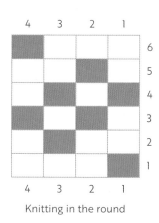

Knitting in the round

Colourwork charts usually only show a single pattern motif (in this case four stitches) and not the actual number of stitches in the row. You then repeat the motif as many times as is instructed in the pattern.

NOTE

Technically, both traditional and modern colourwork is knitted in the round, which can be easily represented on a chart. As charts for colourwork in rows are more difficult to follow, they are more unusual.

26

Identifying colours on a chart

First, look at the key and note next to it the colours you are planning to use. As you can see on the chart below, the white square MC represents the main colour, while square CC1 represents contrasting colour number 1. This means that on the first row you should knit a pink stitch (CC1) followed by three white stitches (MC).

Generally, the colours in the diagram are the same as those used in the project shown in the photograph. Sometimes, however, the different colours are illustrated by different shades of grey. In all cases, each shade of grey represents a particular yarn colour, and these will be specified in the instructions. We will look at how to choose the right colours in Chapter 5.

MC
CC1

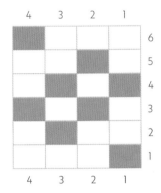

NOTE

The key is usually given either immediately next to the chart or in the abbreviations on the last page of the pattern, book or catalogue.

Understanding increases and decreases

If, when it comes to your motif, the number of stitches is not the same throughout your work, the increases and/or decreases will be shown on the chart. For example, in the case of a hat knitted from bottom to top (from the ribbing to the crown of the hat), you will see decreases mentioned.

By contrast, for a sweater that is knitted from top to bottom (neck down), you will be instructed to work increases at specific points.

Increases and decreases that are not worked in as part of the colourwork motif are not referred to on the chart but in the pattern instructions.

Let us look at an example. Here is the start of a colourwork chart for a sweater **knitted from top to bottom**. There are a certain number of stitches at the start for the yoke. Increases are then worked progressively to achieve the circumference you want for the shoulders. You read the chart **from bottom to top**, always from right to left (knitted in the round).

On rows 1 and 2, numerous stitches are not yet present: they are represented by the grey boxes saying 'No stitch'. So you only need to knit the five stitches in the main colour, and repeat that until the end of the row (so the whole row is knitted in the main colour).

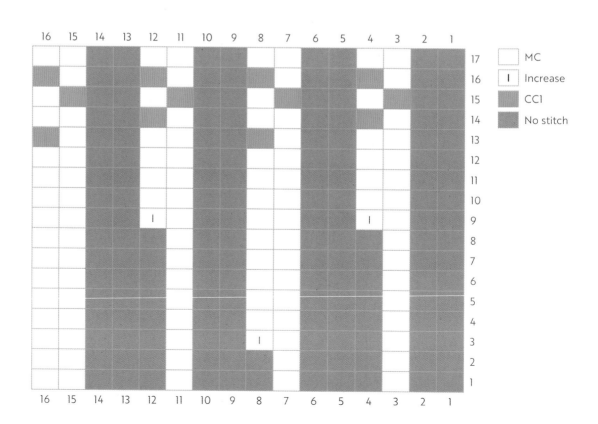

Row 3 has an increase box and reads as follows: knit two stitches (the two white ones that appear first), work an increase (box I), then knit three stitches (white boxes). Repeat this across the whole row.

On the next row (row 4), a grey box has disappeared in line with the stitch created in the previous row.

The principle is the same when the number of stitches decreases.

In the second example below, still starting from the bottom right-hand corner, this time you are very quickly into the colourwork, which is around the shoulders.

In this case, the key includes the boxes 'k2tog' and 'ssk', which are two types of decreases (respectively, knit two stitches together, and slip two stitches one after the other – see page 136).

In row 11, for example, you will work a decrease, knit a stitch in the main colour, work two consecutive decreases, knit three stitches and work a final decrease. The four stitches removed by the decreases are now represented by the four grey boxes that appear in this row.

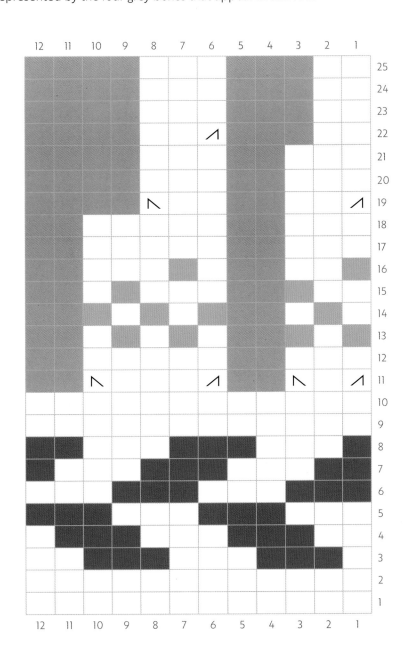

Depending on which patterns or software you use, the charts can differ slightly, but the idea is always the same.

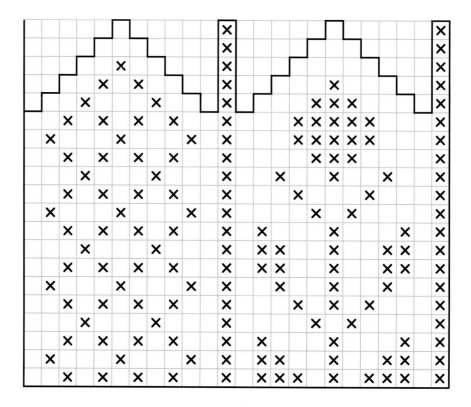

This part of the chart represents the thumb of a traditional Norwegian mitten. As you can see, there are no row numbers, crosses, rather than a coloured square, are used to signal the contrasting colour and there are no grey 'no stitch' squares, but rather a black line outlining the shape of the work and showing where there are stitch decreases.

The idea is nonetheless the same as with a more detailed diagram, as we see in this example.

From row 1 to 15 (reading from bottom to top and from right to left), you simply need to work your stitches swapping between the main colour (white square) and the contrasting colour (square with a cross). You knit 24 stitches for 15 rows.

In row 16, you will start to work decreases to give the thumb its rounded shape. You will knit one stitch, work one decrease (a white square disappears), knit nine stitches, work one decrease, knit one stitch, work a decrease, knit nine stitches, work one decrease. Now you have worked four decreases in the row and your stitch count has gone down from 24 to 20.

You continue in the same way.

By the end of row 20, only four stitches remain.

How to follow the rows while knitting

Following the colours on the chart while keeping an eye on yarn changes and tension (gauge) can sometimes be quite a juggling act. Here are a few tricks that will make reading the chart a little easier. It is up to you to decide which you prefer.

Before you begin

+ Use a photocopier to **enlarge your colourwork chart** if you find the one in the pattern too small. Make it big enough to prop on a table or sofa. This will allow you to knit comfortably without having to pick up the chart too often to check the motif and ensure you are not confusing the rows.

+ If the colours you have chosen are significantly different from the colours used in the project, **print the chart in black and white and colour in the boxes in colours similar to the ones you are going to use**. This will lead to fewer knitting errors.

+ If your chart is large, take a pen and **draw a vertical line on your chart every 10 stitches. It will be easier to follow the blocks of 10 stitches** rather than entire rows to be repeated.

+ When you knit, **add markers to divide the different sequences**. This allows you to check regularly that you have not gone wrong and you can compare stitches with the previous sequence.

Colour in the line you have just knitted with a marker pen.

Using masking/paper tape to cover the lines you have knitted.

While you are knitting

+ **Colour in the line you have just knitted with a marker pen.** This will ensure that you never repeat it again by mistake. I always use this little trick as it means I can identify clearly where I have got to. Watch out though: if you make a mistake and have to undo a few rows, you cannot remove the colour you have added and you might find yourself getting lost.

+ **The moving sticky note technique:** there is nothing simpler to keep track of where you have got to on a chart. Once you have knitted the row, cover it with the sticky note so it cannot be confused with the next row. This trick is ideal if you have to unravel some rows and go back a few stages. However, it may be difficult to find a sticky note big enough to cover the whole line, depending on the size of your chart. This technique works just as well if you are reading your pattern on a tablet.

+ **The use of masking/paper tape** is my top trick. Cut a strip of tape the same length as the line in your diagram and stick it over the line once you have completed that row. Then you have two choices: either cover each row with a different strip or move your strip as your knitting progresses. Use very low-tack tape to ensure you don't tear your paper. This technique works just as well if you are reading from a tablet.

+ **Magnetic board:** if you have one of these, they are very handy for displaying your colourwork chart. Place it on the board and use a magnetic strip to cover the row you have just completed. Move it as you progress.

CHAPTER 4

Choosing a project according to difficulty

We all have different ideas when it comes to what we want to make. In addition, as beginners we do not all approach difficulty in the same way; some people might quickly feel out of their depth if the chart for their knit is a little too complex, while others might get bored if what they are doing is not sufficiently challenging. You know what sort of person you are: do what suits you and not something that will put you off.

My tips on choosing your project wisely

It is often said that it is easier to start colourwork with a hat than a larger garment. I actually started with a hat and, to be honest, I found the process complex. Attempting to achieve an even tension (gauge) over a small circumference was trickier for me than over a bigger one such as for a child's sweater. As a result, I would advise you not to trust blindly what you might read, but to do what you want to do. Just because you begin colourwork with a garment does not mean it will be more complicated. It is rather the choice of colourwork chart that will determine the level of difficulty.

With colourwork, you can knit with one, two, three or even ten contrasting colours. But one of the best pieces of advice I can give to beginners is to choose a pattern that has no more than two colours in any given row. It is much trickier juggling with three colours (and so three balls of yarn) in a single row when you have not yet found the best way of achieving even tension (gauge) with only two!

It is important to remember at this point that knitting colourwork in several colours is not necessarily more complicated: it will only be more complicated if the rows involve more than two colours at the same time.

Some colourwork patterns are classified as difficult because the motif means you need to carry your yarn across the back of the knit very evenly to retain an even tension (gauge) (note that when there are numerous consecutive stitches in a single colour, the non-working yarn is left on the wrong side of the knit until you need it, using a technique that we will tackle in Chapter 8). I would recommend that you only attempt these knits once you have sufficient experience under your belt. At the end of the day, while blocking will even out your knit, you cannot really rectify a tight tension (gauge) problem once the project is finished.

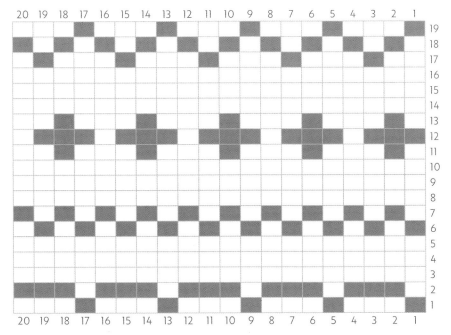

Peerie motif chart.

When you are alternating rows of peerie with rows of larger motifs, the tension (gauge) is more constant across the colourwork and the knit is easier to work. ('Peerie' is a Scottish word meaning 'small' that refers to rows of small colourwork motifs, generally across one to seven rows.) By contrast, a design that has several rows of colourwork, interspersed by numerous rows in the main colour, before a few final rows of colourwork, may result in tension (gauge) differences between the plain and the colourwork. This may not look great, especially if you are new to this technique.

Make sure you do not take on too many challenges simultaneously, and try out the different techniques one by one or two by two! If you are throwing yourself into your first colourwork and your first sweater at the same time, don't add the steek technique into the mix (this is the technique that allows you to turn a sweater into a cardigan – see Chapter 10) unless you are feeling particularly adventurous!

Choose a sweater where the design is around the bottom rather than on the yoke if you are nervous about knitting increases or decreases at the same time as colourwork. Ensure that you have tools such as thread guides to help you (we will discuss them in more detail in Chapter 8).

Once you have got to grips with the colourwork technique and your tension (gauge) is even, you can then tackle more complex colourwork with three colours in a single row.

Tip

Before you begin, knit a swatch to test your tension. If you are a beginner, this will also allow you to gauge the complexity of the knit and see whether it is to your taste.

The projects featured in this book have been created at varying levels of difficulty, from beginner to more advanced:

+ **The Blisco hat – see page 108** (children's and adults' sizes): although starting with a hat is not necessarily the simplest option, this pattern is intended for people who want to get going with something quick. It is knitted in the round, with simple colourwork (no more than two colours per row and no need to strand your yarn on the back, other than on the last two rows) and the decreases are worked after you have finished the colourwork.

+ **The Helvellyn sweater – see page 112** (children's sizes): with the colourwork positioned as a border around the bottom of the sweater, you will not need to manage your tension (gauge) at the same time as working decreases or increases. In addition, as there are only two colours per row and you do not have to strand your yarn across the back, this knit will suit both beginners and more advanced knitters.

+ **The Bowfell sweater – see page 117** (women's sizes): this pattern has been designed to be accessible to beginners but with a motif that will be of interest to more advanced knitters as well. It is knitted in the round, with no more than two colours per row and no need to strand your yarn across the back. This sweater is a great starter project if you are doing colourwork for an adult for the first time.

+ **The Scafell sweater – see page 124** (women's sizes): this pattern is the most complex in the book and seeks to offer knitters who have already tried colourwork some new challenges. The motif comprises up to three colours per row but you do not need to strand your yarn across the back.

+ **The Scafell cardigan – see page 130** (women's sizes): this cardigan version of the previous knit is an opportunity to try out the steek technique; it is not too complicated, but people are often nervous about it. If you do not feel up to trying it straight away, I would advise you to start with the sweater version.

Helvellyn and Bowfell sweaters.

Scafell cardigan and Blisco hat.

CHAPTER 5

Choosing your colours

The appeal of colourwork lies in knitting with several different colours. However, to ensure an attractive result, the colours should not be chosen at random. This preparation stage often takes time, but, in my opinion, the planning is also an interesting part of the process.

The colour wheel

When you decide to knit with several colours, take your time in selecting the right ones to ensure that the end result lives up to your expectations.

The first thing to look at when you are choosing colours is the famous colour wheel. This wheel is a good starting point to prevent you getting lost in the huge array of possible colours! It allows you to organize colours depending on where they are located on the spectrum and to understand how the different colours relate to each other.

There are a number of ways of choosing colours on the wheel:

+ **Choose opposing colours (also known as complementary colours)** on the wheel, by drawing a straight line through the centre to link the two (see the photos below): so you could select green and pink, red and blue, or even a pink and sky blue.

+ **Choose neighbouring colours (also known as analogous colours):** pink and mauve, dark blue and light blue, red and orange. However, analogous colours must be well contrasted for the pattern to show up.

+ **Choose a triad of colours,** if you need to pick three contrasting colours: draw a triangle on the colour wheel and choose one colour from each corner – for example, red-blue-green or purple-orange-light blue.

 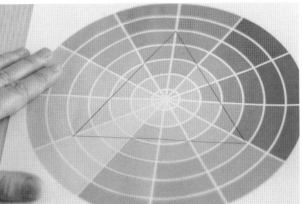

Contrast

Contrast between colours is the second criteria to take into account when selecting your yarns. It is particularly important if you are choosing shades that are relatively similar. If you decide to knit with two blues, for example, it is essential that they are as contrasting as possible, such as a dark blue and a light blue. This is equally true if you opt for a neutral colour (white, grey, black). If the contrast is not sufficiently marked, the colours will merge and the motif will not stand out.

NOTE

If you go for a hand-dyed yarn with colour variations, it is possible that it might only contrast for a few centimetres and the rest will merge into the main colour. I would advise choosing a plain colour with no variations when using this sort of wool.

Choosing colours according to the pattern

Another very important point to consider when selecting your colours is the number of colour groups present in the chosen pattern.

Take, for example, the Riddari sweater by Védís Jónsdóttir (see top left): it has a main colour (white), a background colour just for the colourwork section (royal blue) then two contrasting colours that are knitted only with the background colour. It is therefore essential to choose colours that contrast with the background colour (royal blue) and not with the main colour of the knit!

The background colour (royal blue) contrasts sufficiently with the main colour (white) to ensure that the general colourwork pattern is nice and clear. The other contrasting colours (turquoise and mustard) in turn contrast very well with the background colour (royal blue). As a result, the colourwork stands out perfectly on this sweater.

By contrast, my Marieke women's sweater (see bottom left) has no background colour on the colourwork section. As a result, all the colours of the motif must contrast with the sweater's main colour, here, white. It is fairly easy to find contrasting colours: just choose relatively dark colours so the design stands out clearly.

On the other hand, if you decide to opt for a dark colour as the main colour for a pattern of this type, you must use light colours for the motif. If, however, you are keen to combine dark colours, just make sure the different shades are a long way apart on the colour wheel.

Choosing your colours step by step

The first step can be done at home, when you are thinking about your choice of colours. The second and third steps can be done in the yarn shop. Study the different shades next to each other, following the guidance given below before buying your yarn. Finally, the last step, the swatch, will be something you do at home, but make sure you have a plan B for your colours as it is not unusual to decide to change your first choice.

1 Use the colour wheel and contrast

I would recommend that you start with the colour wheel, and on the basis of the colours that appeal to you, follow the different techniques described on pages 42–43. Next, give consideration to contrast, especially if you have opted to start off with analogous colours (close to each other on the wheel).

2 Take a black-and-white photo

Here is a tip that I was given when I was on a colourwork course in Montreal at the start of my knitting journey, which I have used numerous times since:

Before you make a final decision on your colours and start your swatch, take the different skeins or balls that you have selected for your project and put them on a table under natural light. Then take a picture of them next to each other, in the same order as the knit colours, if possible. Display your photo in black and white on your phone or tablet. You can then get a good idea of the contrast between the colours.

This trick means you are not wholly reliant on your own judgement of the balls, because once they are knitted together, the result might really be quite different from what you had imagined. If two colours appear very similar, or indeed identical in black and white, this means that they are too close and risk merging once knitted. For example, in the photos below, you can see that the blue and ecru are still a good contrast in black and white, whereas the pink and ecru look very similar.

45

❸ Twisting the yarns together

Another technique that works well when you have to choose two colours is to twist your yarns together. This allows you to see whether the colours blend into each other (see below, left) or if they contrast sufficiently (see below, right).

❹ The swatch

Once you have settled on your colours, it is essential to knit a pattern swatch to try them together. If you launch straight into your project and then realize that the colours do not work well together, you will have to unravel it all, and undoing colourwork is not easy. The swatch stage really will make your life easier. Don't hesitate to select a wide range of colours and experiment with different combinations in your swatches. (See pages 50–57 on knitting a swatch in the round.)

Opting for a pre-prepared yarn kit

Nowadays, colourwork pattern designers often collaborate with yarn brands to offer kits all ready for you to knit. Sometimes it is the dyers themselves who offer kits for sale for specific patterns. Generally speaking, these kits include the pattern (or not) as well as the yardage of yarn required to knit the project.

So, is this solution worth considering if you are uncertain of success when it comes to choosing your initial colours? It usually is, as the yarns have been pre-selected for you. However, I have two recommendations to make if you are choosing this option:

+ Ask to see knitted swatches and/or examples of the pattern knitted in these yarns. You need to make sure that colours go well together and do not merge into each other when knitted up. Don't forget the colour and contrast wheel principles discussed on pages 42–43. The same principles apply here, even if it is a dyer who has created the kits.

+ Opt for kits where the quantity of yarn matches the pattern and your chosen size. By doing so, you are paying only for what you really need and won't be left with barely used skeins at the end of your project.

CHAPTER 6

Knitting a swatch in the round

The swatch is a very important stage when you are embarking on colourwork, particularly in the round. In this chapter, we will take a detailed look at what swatches are used for and how you knit them.

What is a swatch?

This is an essential building block for a successful knit. The swatch means you can test the yarn (look, thickness, quality) and tension (gauge) (the number of stitches and rows over 10cm [4in], which allows you to check the final size of the knit), but above all, it allows you to confirm or reconsider your choice of colours.

The swatch can be done in rows or in the round. It is important to remember that your tension (gauge) may be totally different depending on the type of knit, namely whether it is in rows or in the round with no seams. In the round, you only use knit stitch, while if you are knitting in rows, you alternate a row of knit with a row of purl.

Make sure you knit a swatch in rows if your knit is to be in rows, and in the round if your knit is to be in the round.

Some people find the idea of knitting a swatch tedious if they are champing at the bit to get going on their knit, but it is well worth the time you spend on it. If your tension (gauge) is different from the tension (gauge) given on your pattern, it will have a direct impact on the measurements of the knit, which could then be a lot larger or smaller than the one you were expecting at the start. This can be a real problem if you are knitting an item of clothing, for example.

KNITTING TENSION (GAUGE)

The tension (gauge) is the result of the way the knitter holds the yarn, whether tightly or loosely, at the time of knitting.

It is measured on the basis of the number of stitches and rows over a 10 x 10cm (4 x 4in) swatch. The swatch allows you to calculate whether your knit will end up the same size as the pattern.

Two people knitting the same pattern with the same yarn and the same size needles may not have the same tension (gauge) and so will not necessarily obtain the same swatch.

Tension (gauge) is especially important for colourwork because the fact that you are using several yarns in a single row can have a major impact. This is less the case in plain stocking (stockinette) stitch where you are using a single yarn.

In stranded colourwork, the fact that you carry the non-working yarn across the back of your work has a tendency to pull on the knit and make it less elastic. The first difficulty in colourwork is to find the right tension (gauge). This means knitting evenly throughout, even though you are using different yarns. People's first attempts at colourwork are often too tight and this makes for a uneven finish which will not flatten out after washing. It is thus recommended to knit more loosely. We will take a closer look at some techniques and tips for ensuring good colourwork tension (gauge) in Chapter 9.

Making a swatch in the round

There are two different techniques for knitting a swatch in the round: either by working only in knit stitch and using floats, or by working a tube in the round. Both techniques are described in more detail on the following pages. I prefer the first but would recommend that you try both and pick the one you like best.

When you knit a colourwork swatch, it is important to knit several repeats of the motif, or parts of the motif, so you can check the tension (gauge), the finished appearance of the yarn and the colours.

Tip

To knit a swatch (especially if you are using the first technique), cast on more stitches than you would expect for 10cm (4in) because the two-to-three stitches at the edges tend to have a looser tension (gauge) than those in the middle. So, cast on the equivalent of 15 x 15cm (6 x 6in) of stitches so you can then count the number of stitches over a 10 x 10cm (4 x 4in) square in the middle.

Left: tube swatch; right: swatch with floats.

Knitting with floats

For this technique, cast on several repeats of your motif so it is wider than 10cm (4in) plus two additional stitches on each side for your border. For example: if your motif is 14 stitches, cast on 32 (2 motifs + 4 border stitches). If your motif is 6 stitches, cast on 28 (4 motifs + 4 border stitches).

Tip

You can hold your yarn behind to make sure it is loose enough.

Work a row in knit stitch. Then on the next row, instead of turning over your swatch to knit a purl row as you would for a flat swatch, slide your stitches along the cable on to the other needle and start knitting again with another row of knit stitch. As the working yarn (the yarn attached to the ball) remains on the left, you have to leave a sufficient length, or 'float' at the back to ensure the swatch is not stretched and does not pull on the stitches. Work a second row in knit stitch. Repeat until you have a swatch of a sufficient size, ideally 15cm (6in), so you can then measure the number of rows across a distance of 10cm (4in).

1. Cast on and work a row in knit stitch.

2. Slide the stitches round the cable on to the other needle.

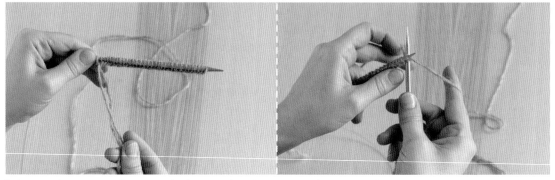

3. Leave a long piece of yarn on the back before knitting the first stitch of the new row. You can hold it in your non-dominant hand to stop it from pulling.

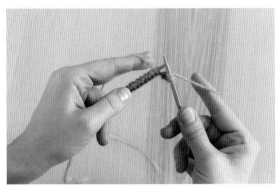

4. Work the row in knit stitch.

5. When you have finished this next row, slide the stitches round to the other needle and continue in the same way for the whole swatch.

6. Add the new colour when required, to form the motif.

Note: the yarn in the contrasting colour must always be trapped in the first and last stitch of the row so it is held in place.

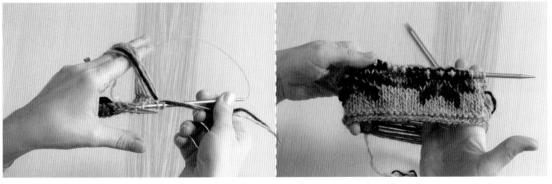

7. Check that the floats of yarn at the back are long enough to ensure that they do not pull on the motif.

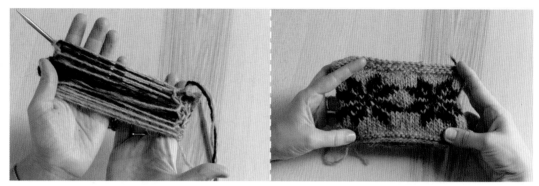

And there you have it! The photo above, left, shows the yarn floats on the back of the swatch; the photo on the right shows the swatch from the front.

MY EXPERIENCE

When I first starting knitting, I always took the time to work a swatch in the round if my project was done in the round and in rows if the project was a cardigan, scarf or similar. With experience, I realized that my tension (gauge) was identical in both cases. As a result, I only do swatches in the round when it is a colourwork knit and I want to try out the motif and colours.

By contrast, some people might find a difference of three or four stitches between a swatch in rows and one in rounds – this will have a direct impact on the size of the finished project. It is therefore worth taking the time to assess how you knit in rows and in the round, before deciding that the flat swatches are quicker and easier to do.

Knitting a tube

Note that for a tube swatch you will be making a swatch that is twice as big as the measurements given in the pattern, since once it is laid flat, your tube will be folded in half. Consequently, if the pattern recommends a certain number of stitches for a 10cm (4in) swatch (which is generally the case), your tube must measure at least 20cm (8in), or indeed a little more, so you can measure and count the stitches or rows over the required 10cm (4in) on one width of the tube.

This swatch technique has the advantage of being faithful to what you will knit subsequently (because it is totally in the round) but it requires more yarn and more time than the first technique. In this case, as it is only a small diameter, you have the choice of knitting it using the magic loop technique or with 23cm (9in) or 30cm (11¾in) circular needles.

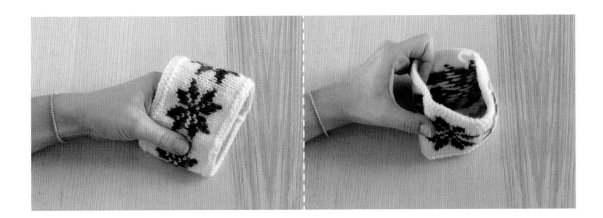

My advice

If you are knitting in a magic loop, change the spot where you are dividing your stitches in half occasionally so that you don't have a visible separation on the right side where the two parts separate. This advice applies as much to your actual knit as to your swatch.

As with the flat swatch, I would advise you to work a garter stitch border at the bottom and top of the swatch to prevent it from rolling up.

Blocking and measuring the swatch

You must block (e.g. soak and pin out) then measure your swatch once it is dry so you can use it to calculate the exact number of stitches necessary for 10cm (4in). Start by immersing your swatch in a basin of cold or lukewarm water with a bit of laundry detergent and leave for around 30 minutes. Squeeze dry in a towel and lay flat to dry. You can pin it to hold the edges in place, but ensure that you are not stretching it.

Once it is dry, count the number of stitches over a 10cm (4in) width and the number of rows over a height of 10cm (4in).

Tip

For a swatch knitted using the floats method (method one), it is best to cut the yarn floats once you have taken the swatch out of the water and while it is still damp.

Run some lukewarm water in the sink and put in some laundry detergent.

Immerse your swatch in the soapy water.

Dry your swatch in a towel, then place it on a blocking mat.

Cut the extra yarn at the back of your swatch.

Lay your swatch flat on the mat.

Pin the sides of the swatch and allow to dry.

The swatch, once dry.

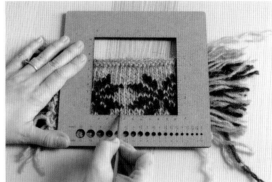

Count the number of stitches within 10cm (4in) to get the tension (gauge).

CHAPTER 7

Intarsia colourwork

Unlike stranded colourwork, with this technique you do not need to carry your yarn across the back of the work because it is used to work a single motif that is not repeated along the row.

Techniques and tricks

It is generally easiest to do intarsia colourwork in rows, alternating knit and purl rows. Each coloured section is knitted with a different ball.

For example, in the photo (below): the right hand part is knitted with a white ball (A1), the heart with a red ball (B1) while the part on the left of the heart is knitted with another white ball (A2). Therefore, you need three balls to work this motif on the lower rows and five balls for the upper rows (three white and two red). The numbers, which alternate from left to right of the chart, indicate that the knit is worked in rows.

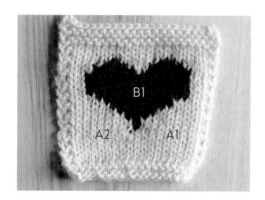

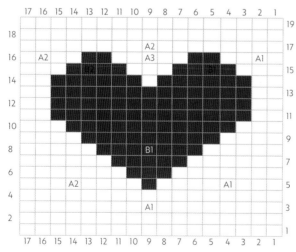

There are many tricky aspects to intarsia knitting: the number of yarns you use, the balls of wool that tend to get mixed up and the little holes that can form when you change colour. The more colours you use for your motif, the more complicated things become.

Intarsia in rows

For intarsia colourwork in rows, follow your chart as you would for stranded colourwork in rows, i.e. read even rows from right to left and odd rows from left to right.

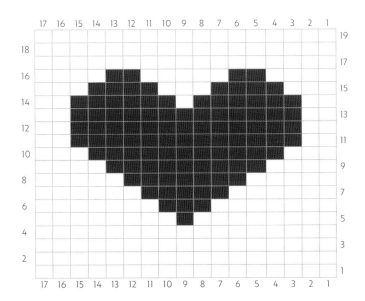

However, unlike stranded colourwork, remember that here, each coloured section involves a different ball of yarn.

Right side

Right side

Wrong side

The main difficulty with intarsia colourwork is changing colour: if it is done badly, a hole can form, or the opposite, the stitches can be too tight. On the following pages are the steps you should follow to knit this type of colourwork.

Tutorial

Knit row

1. Prepare the number of balls you will need to knit your motif.

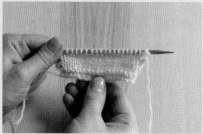

2. Start knitting normally with yarn A1 until the first stitch in the contrasting colour.

3. Add the contrasting yarn, leaving a long enough tail for you to be able to work it in at the end (B1).

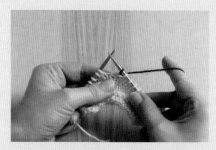

4. Knit your stitch with this contrasting yarn: here, the base of the heart.

5. Now you are going to use white again, but because it is intarsia, you will use a different ball of white to knit the next part (A2).

6. Add the new white yarn (A2).

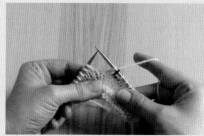

7. Knit with this yarn.

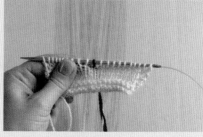

8. Finish the row with this same white yarn (A2).

Purl row

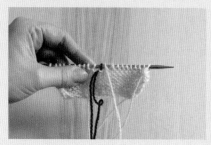

9. Turn your work to start the purl row: the yarn has a tendency to be quite loose at the beginning, so it is fine to pull on it gently to tighten it all up. The shorter yarns will be worked in at the end.

10. Knit your purl row up to the point where it changes colour. At this point, you will have to twist the yarns around each other to fill the hole that will form when you knit with the red.

11. To prevent holes forming when you change colour, twist the yarns around each other by placing the one that you have just used over the new yarn, then working with this new yarn (in this case in purl as you are on the purl row). Do this each time you start knitting in a new colour, even if it has already been used.

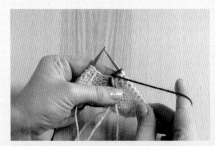

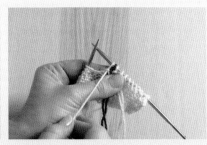

12. Once again, after the red stitch, you must now work a white stitch.

13. Pass the red yarn over the white yarn. Take the white thread underneath and work the stitch in white.

14. Knit with the white yarn until the end of the row.

Knit row

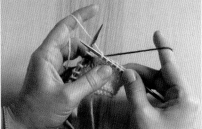

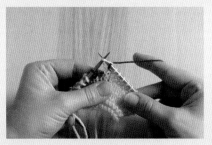

15. Each time you change colour on the knit rows, the yarns should be twisted around each other on the wrong side as previously.

16. The technique is identical: take the previous colour and pass it over the top (here the white yarn); take the new colour and trap it underneath (here the red yarn).

17. Work the stitch in the new colour (red).

Working in the ends of the yarn in flat intarsia

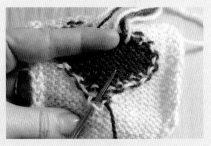

1. When you introduce a colour for the first time, it is normal for a hole to be formed next to it.

2. Use your tapestry needle to work in the tail of yarn.

3. Pass the yarn over the neighbouring white stitch to complete the red stitch.

The red stitch and the white stitch, which were previously separated, are now linked as if it were the same colour without a gap.

Repeat for each new colour/new yarn introduced.

Knitting intarsia in the round

While it is generally simpler to knit intarsia colourwork in rows, knitting it in the round is much more complicated and consequently far less common. When knitting in the round, every row is in knit stitch. This means that, when you go to knit a colour on a new row, the yarn in this colour knitted on the previous row will always be on the other side of the motif because it is not carried over the back as it is in stranded colourwork.

If the motif is small and only across a few rows, you can either strand your yarn behind your motif, or use new yarn for each contrasting colour and for each row.

On the other hand, if the motif is large, there is no solution other than to knit purl rows in order to pick up the yarn at the right place, which is not possible if you are knitting stocking (stockinette) stitch in the round. This is why if you are dead set on knitting in the round, the best method to use would be the short row method (otherwise known as 'wrap and turn', see opposite), which will allow you to knit purl rows over part of your work. For the section in short rows, you will not knit in the round but in rows while working the motif. Always try and retain the same tension (gauge).

There are two ways of knitting intarsia in the round:

The short row or wrap and turn method

1. Work the knit row following the chart until the last stitch of the row (the place where you put your marker at the start of the row).

2. Work a short row on the first stitch of the next row: slip the next stitch on the left needle purlwise onto the right needle. The yarn must remain behind the work. Bring the yarn to the front of the work then slip stitch from the right needle back to the left needle. Take the yarn to the back. The stitch is now wrapped.

3. Turn the work over and purl a row in accordance with the colours on the chart until you get to the wrapped stitch.

4. Replace the yarn wrapping the stitch on the needle and knit it with the main stitch.

5. Work a short row on the last stitch of the row: slip the next stitch on the left needle purlwise on to the right needle. Take the yarn to the back of the work. Replace the slipped stitch on the left needle and bring the yarn to the front. The stitch is now wrapped.

6. Turn the work over and work in knit stitch again.

   Continue using this technique until you have worked your whole intarsia motif, following the colours on your pattern chart. Once you have finished your motif, start knitting in the round again normally.

Yarn over method

1. Yarn over at the start of the first row of intarsia and knit this row to the end following the colour chart.

2. Ssk (slip 1 stitch, slip 1 stitch, knit these two stitches together with the yarn behind) with the last stitch of the row and the slipped stitch.

3. Turn your work over, yarn over and purl your row to the end.

4. Purl two stitches together taking the last stitch of the row and the yarn over.

   This technique is similar to the previous one but less visible because of the yarn over and decreases.

AN ALTERNATIVE TO INTARSIA: DUPLICATE STITCHES

If you want to add only a few colour stitches to your garment, accessory or children's toy, you do not necessarily have to knit intarsia.

In this case, you can use the duplicate stitches method, as long as you use wool of the same thickness as the wool you are using for the main knit.

This technique is explained in detail in Chapter 9 (see page 84).

CHAPTER 8

Stranded colourwork

In this chapter we will take a closer look at the techniques you need to know for knitting stranded colourwork. You will then have all the knowledge you need to get started.

Holding your yarn

There are various ways of holding your yarn, none of them right or wrong. The most important thing is to settle on the technique that you find most comfortable and that will allow you to achieve a good tension (gauge). It is worth trying several different methods and taking the time to experiment.

With two yarns

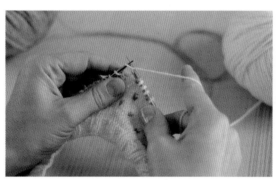 

Two yarns to the right, 'classic' style: this technique is often used by newcomers to colourwork knitting. The two yarns are positioned to the right and knitted one after the other according to the chart. The advantage of this method is that it is simple and you do not have to learn to manage the tension (gauge) in the same way as you do with the continental method (one yarn in each hand). However, it takes longer, because you have to keep dropping the first yarn and taking up the second one and vice versa; the repetitive motion can also lead to shoulder pains.

One yarn in each hand, 'continental' style: if you already knit in the continental style with a single colour, or you want to learn a good method for knitting colourwork immediately, I recommend you hold one yarn in each hand. This method is speedy and less painful on the shoulders because it requires less movement.

Two yarns to the left: this technique can be used by knitters who are comfortable with the continental method. However, for colourwork beginners, it might be preferable to hold one yarn in each hand. It is important to position your yarns well, respecting the order of colour dominance (see later in the chapter) and holding each yarn with a different finger. You can then knit in the continental style, alternating the yarns to be worked in accordance with the chart.

With three yarns

One yarn to the left and two yarns to the right: when you knit in this style, you use your left hand as you would in the continental style and your right hand as you would in the 'classic' style. When you change the yarn on the right, you have to drop your colour each time to pick up the other.

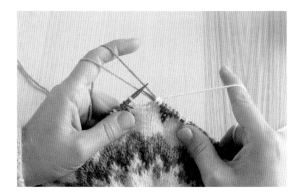

Two yarns to the left and one to the right: in this case you always keep the same colour in your right hand, but it is the yarn in your left hand that changes. At the point shown on the pattern chart, you pick up the pink with your right-hand needle; if you need to work the yellow, you pick up the yellow with the right-hand needle.

Using a thread guide

The thread guide makes it easier for you to pick up the yarns on the left when you are knitting in the continental style, because they are easier to distinguish than when they are held over your finger. The thread guide also helps to maintain better tension (gauge).

Using a plastic thread guide

Separate the yarns.

Place the two left-hand yarns on the guide.

Hold the right-hand yarn in your right hand.

Knit the stitches.

Using a metal thread guide

Put the guide on your finger.

Position your fingers.

Knit a stitch (here, pink).

Introducing a new colour

Knitting with several colours means that you will have to introduce a new yarn into your work. This stage is very simple. You do not need to knot the yarns together, just leave around 3cm (1¼in) of yarn and start immediately with the new colour at the point required. The tails of yarn will be worked in using a tapestry needle at the finishing stage, when the work is complete.

Respecting colour dominance

Colour dominance is a complex matter and its importance varies depending on the type of colourwork and the country or region of the people who knit it. Some think it is an essential consideration while others believe it to have no impact on the final look of a knit.

But what is colour dominance in the colourwork context?

When you are working in stranded colourwork, the colours will stand out differently depending on how the yarns are arranged on the back of the work: it is, therefore, something that can be dictated depending on the way you hold the yarns while working.

For a two-colour knit, when the background colour and motif colour are worked in the same row, the stitches in one of the two colours look bigger, and more dominant, than the stitches in the other colour.

On the example below, the dominance has been reversed between the left mitten and the right mitten.

On the right hand, it is the contrasting colour, the red, that has been held as the dominant colour, and the main colour, grey, which has been held as the non-dominant. As a result, the red yarns on the wrong side of the work show through more (longer strands underneath) and the motif stands out better on the right side.

By contrast, on the left mitten, it is the grey yarn (main colour) that has been held as the dominant, while the red yarn (contrasting) has been held as the non-dominant. The result is that, on the wrong side, it is the grey thread that strands underneath and which stands out the most. On the right side, the red motif stands out less than on the right mitten.

Consequently, it is advisable to hold the contrasting colour as the dominant colour to make it stand out against the main colour.

Look closely at the mittens above. Do you notice any difference between the two pairs? The mittens on the right in the above images had red held as the dominant colour, while the mittens on the left had grey held as the dominant colour.

Take a look at this next example (the Blisco hat), and you can see that the main colour (blue) becomes the contrasting colour halfway up the hat.

At the start of the knit (from the ribbing to halfway up the motif), when the main colour was blue, the white was held as the dominant colour while the blue was held as the non-dominant colour.

These colours have been reversed halfway up the pattern: the blue was then held as the dominant colour and the white non-dominant. This means that on the right side, the white contrasting motif stands out well at the bottom of the hat, while the blue contrasting motif then stands out better at the top.

On the back, you can see that the positioning of the yarns changes too. Below the level of the pencil, the blue yarn is stranded over the top, while above the pencil, the white yarn is on top and the blue yarn underneath.

Tip

In my experience, it is important to take colour dominance into account. I find that it has a direct impact on the extent to which your motif will stand out.

IMPORTANT SUMMARY

Colour dominance will be different depending on how you work your yarns: **the one that is stranded under the other will stand out more and be the dominant colour**. The one that 'floats' over the other will be less perceptible, or non-dominant. Choose the colour that you want to stand out the most and strand it underneath.

Holding your yarn to respect colour dominance

If you are knitting in the continental style, hold the main colour (background or non-dominant colour) in your right hand and the contrasting colour (dominant) in your left hand.

If you are knitting with both yarns in your left hand, the yarn the furthest to the left will be the dominant one.

Contrasting colour (dominant) to the left, main colour (non-dominant) to the right.

The finish on the wrong side is even.

Tip

Once you have chosen the dominant colour for your project, and if your main colour is the same throughout, continue to hold your yarns in the same way so that the dominance remains constant throughout the knit.

Even if some people do not find colour dominance important to the final look of the project, in my opinion, it makes the inside of the knit look good: the yarns are always positioned in the same place, which makes the wrong side neat and even.

TRICK

So you don't get the colours mixed up, and to ensure that your dominant colour remains constant, place your balls of wool on either side of your work and keep them like that until your knit is finished. This will also mean you never get your yarns in a tangle.

Stranding your yarn across the back

One of the specific characteristics of stranded colourwork, which distinguishes it from other types of coloured knits (such as intarsia), is that the non-working yarn is stranded across the wrong side of the work. These strands are also known as floats.

If a colour is not worked for more than seven stitches, the yarn must be trapped in the working yarn so that it floats across the wrong side of the work and allows you to maintain an even tension (gauge). Opinions are divided on the question of whether or not to anchor strands on the wrong side.

+ Traditional Fair Isle knitters do not generally anchor strands on the back because colour changes between motifs are much more frequent than in more modern colourwork motifs. This renders it unnecessary. In addition, traditionally used yarns have a tendency to felt slightly: the strands on the back adhere together and give a unified, consistent finish to the knitted wool after it has been washed.

+ Knitters following colourwork patterns that do not abide by traditional Fair Isle rules and who do not necessarily use 100 per cent natural yarns will tend to anchor their strands on the wrong side. Opinions differ on how often this should be done: some say no more than three stitches should be knitted without anchoring, others five and others seven. It will depend on the weight of the wool, the motif and also what you are making: long floats will be more annoying on mittens than on the yoke of a jumper, for example.

Tip

When I first started knitting colourwork, I felt the need to anchor my yarn every three stitches so the finish on the back would not be too tight. With time and experience I started to do it every five stitches and now I leave seven.

Don't be tempted to skip this stage, especially if you are a beginner, because if your yarn is not anchored regularly on the back of your knit, you risk pulling it too tight. This will have an impact on the tension (gauge) and the final outcome of your project. In addition, if your floats are too long, you might catch your jewellery in them when putting on your garment (sweater sleeves, mittens, and so on).

ALIGNING COLOURS AT THE START OF A ROW

When you are knitting in the round, the end of row 1 and the start of row 2 will be offset by a few millimetres. If you are knitting stocking (stockinette) stitch in a single colour, this cannot be seen at all. However, if you are knitting colourwork or stripes, it will be visible. Patterns with a circular, colourwork yoke generally start the row at the back, on the right shoulder so that the colour changes are less obvious. However there are two simple methods for aligning the colours.

+ **Adjust the tension (gauge):** knit the last stitch of the row in the main colour slightly more loosely, then knit the first stitch of the following row with the contrasting colour slightly more tightly. Playing with the tension (gauge) means you can adjust the height of the rows and this will smooth out nicely at the blocking stage.

+ **Knit two stitches together:** start the row with the new colour and knit the whole row. On the first stitch of the next row, pick up the stitch from the row below (same colour as the stitch above), place it on the left-hand needle and knit these two stitches together.

Tutorial

Two yarns on the left

Take the yarn you want to anchor and twist it around the working yarn.

Continue working with the MC yarn.

The burgundy yarn is now anchored at the back of the work.

One yarn in each hand

Wrap the pink yarn (the one to be anchored), held in your left hand, around the right-hand needle.

Knit the stitch with the yarn held in your right hand.

The pink yarn is now anchored at the back of the work.

CHAPTER 9

Managing yarn tension (gauge)

The biggest difficulty with colourwork (after choosing colours) is achieving a good tension (gauge), given that this technique involves working with several yarns at the same time. In addition, the resulting colourwork is often not as stretchy as simple stocking (stockinette) stitch because of the strands floated across the back of the work, which are themselves not very stretchy.

Finding the right tension (gauge)

Several factors can influence your tension (gauge) when you are knitting colourwork:

+ the type of yarn used: as mentioned in Chapter 2, cotton, for example, is not nearly as stretchy as wool;

+ the type of needles you use (circular or double-pointed);

+ the way you hold your yarn (tightly or loosely);

+ how you strand the yarn on the back of the work (anchoring every three, five or seven stitches).

Good tension (gauge): the work can often create bumps (which will disappear on blocking) but the floats behind are even and stretchy. The work on the wrong side is flat.

Poor tension (gauge): the yarn is pulled too tightly on the wrong side of the work resulting in an uneven finish. As a result, the contrast colour stitches tend to get lost among the stitches in the main colour. The hat shown on the right is not the expected size and will not be a good fit.

The tension (gauge) on the colourwork in the sweater shown on the right is much too tight compared to the stocking (stockinette) stitch knit of the rest of the sweater. As a result, the colourwork section is different and the bottom of the body is too tight. The difference is too significant to remedy with blocking. The only solution is to unravel and redo the colourwork, using needles a couple of sizes bigger.

TRICKS FOR IMPROVING YOUR TENSION (GAUGE)

+ Consider knitting the colourwork section using a larger size of needle than you would for the rest of the knit.

+ Try to knit a little more loosely than usual. In all cases, avoid as far as possible knitting too tightly as this is the major problem that colourwork beginners encounter.

+ If possible, when you begin, twist the yarn on the back every three to four stitches to reduce the length of the floats on the wrong side. This will give you a looser tension (gauge). With experience your floats can be longer, up to a maximum of seven stitches.

+ While you are knitting, check regularly that your work is stretchy by stopping and pulling it gently widthways. This will allow you to check whether your stranding is too tight or too loose and adjust how you are knitting as a result.

+ Use a thread guide to help. You can hold the yarns in your left hand while knitting in the continental style on this side.

+ If your knitting is still tight, you could try another type of wool (different type or weight).

+ Knit with the right side of the work inwards. This means that the colourwork strands are on the outside, where the circumference of the tube is greater.

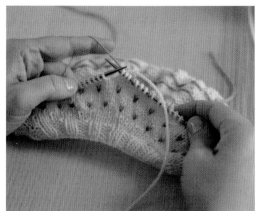 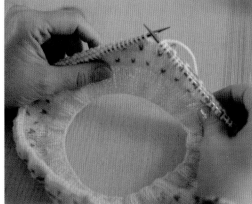

With the right side of the work out.   With the right side of the work in.

Remember that the greatest difficulty with colourwork is getting the tension (gauge) right, and it is perfectly normal not be satisfied with your first attempt.

Small diameters in colourwork

When you are knitting small diameters such as mittens, sleeves or socks, it can be difficult to get good tension (gauge) whether you are using a magic loop or double-pointed needles. The risk is that your tension (gauge) will be too tight on the wrong side where you turn your knit. This then tends to leave a mark that you cannot get rid of by blocking. Consequently, it is very important not to pull your strands too much on the back because if they are too tight, you won't be able the change the tension (gauge) after blocking.

There are several techniques for knitting colourwork over small diameters.

Magic loop

Using a 60–80cm (23½–31½in) cable, it is possible to knit in a magic loop, replacing your stitches regularly so you have no visible separation. When you slide your stitches in the middle of the row, make sure you change the place where you separate one row from another so that there is no line and the yarns do not pull at the back.

Needle placed horizontally during the change

This technique can be used with both circular and double-pointed needles.

When you change sides, place your right needle horizontally, in the same direction as the yarn. By doing this, the yarn behind can be stranded without being pulled tight. The strands on the back will continue to have the same tension (gauge) as the rest of the knit.

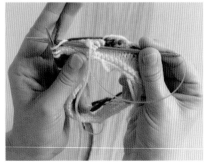
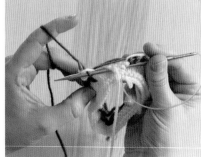
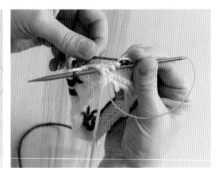

Two pairs of circular needles

To avoid a line of separation and a tension (gauge) problem, you can use two circular needles: one cable for the first half of the stitches and another cable for the other half.

You then have two cables and four needles. Knit the first section of your stitches. When you get to the second part, align the cable of the right-hand needle with the stitches on the left-hand needle and trap it with your thumb. Pull the right-hand and left-hand stitches apart and line them up as if they were on a single needle. Place the yarn that is being stranded to the left and continue knitting. Once the new stitches of the yarn to be stranded have been knitted, you can release the cable. Repeat this technique each time you change sides.

One cable is used to knit the stitches and the other one is positioned horizontally so the yarn behind can be stranded.

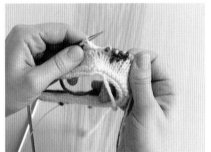

At the separation point, take the second cable and place it horizontally under the working needle, trapping it in place with your thumb.

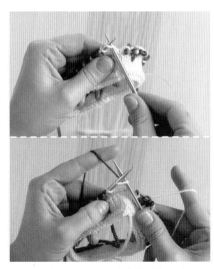

Knit the first stitches while holding the cable horizontally.

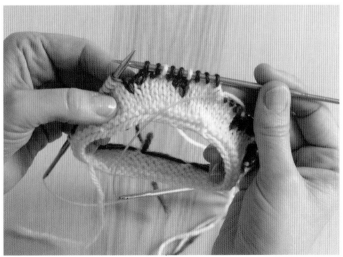

Then release it and continue knitting the row as normal.

Short circular needles

Circular needles of 23cm (9in) or 30cm (11¾in) in length are very practical for knitting small diameters and avoid the need to use a magic loop. Using them allows you to avoid any tension (gauge) problems over small circumferences. However, they are sometimes tricky to hold and so many knitters are not keen on them.

Correcting mistakes

Whether you are just starting out or an experienced knitter, especially with colourwork, you can sometimes encounter tension (gauge) problems or make errors in your motif. Don't panic, this happens to everyone and does not necessarily mean you have to unravel it all.

Tension (gauge) problems

If some of your stitches are too tight and disappear into your background colour, this means your tension (gauge) is too tight and you are not stranding your yarn correctly on the back of your work. To remedy this, simply take your needle and pull the stitch on the right side of the work gently outwards to make it stand out. This technique works when it is just a few stitches, but if a whole row is affected, it is better to undo it.

When the stitches in contrasting colours are bigger than the stitches of the background colour, this means they are knitted more loosely. To make them smaller, you simply need to pull on the strands on the back of the work. You could even then steam-iron your knit (using a wet cloth to protect the wool) so that the stitches stay the right size. It is the same principle for stitches that are too tight: if your row is too loose (although this is rare in colourwork), it is a better idea to unravel.

If the tension (gauge) problem is across the whole row, or indeed over several rows, it is best to undo it. Using the two techniques described above will have an impact on the overall tension (gauge) and resulting look of your knit.

Mistakes in the knitted colours

Correcting while knitting: have you made a mistake with colour on a stitch and only realized at the end of the row? Don't panic – you can correct it on the next row. To do so, continue knitting until you reach the mistake, then slip your needle into the stitch on the previous row as follows: insert the needle from right to left through the stitch, drop the stitch knitted in the wrong colour and place the yarn at the back, then pick up the yarn in the right colour and bring it into your stitch as if you had dropped it. Then replace it the right way round so that it is not twisted and knit it as it is meant to be knitted in your new row.

The stitch in the middle should be grey and not purple.

Knit until you reach the mistake.

Insert the right-hand needle in the stitch of the row below.

Drop the purple yarn with which the stitch is worked on the last row (the mistake).

Pick up the yarn in the right colour from behind (the grey) and put it on the right-hand needle.

Pass the grey stitch over the yarn (as if it were a dropped stitch) and replace it the right way round (so it is not twisted).

You have corrected the error and can continue to knit in accordance with the chart.

Correcting when the knit is finished: have you noticed that some of the stitches are in the wrong colour before blocking your knit? This can be rectified very easily using the **duplicated stitch method**. This technique works best if it is done before blocking. Then, during blocking, all the stitches, including the duplicated ones, can be flattened out and the mistakes will not be noticeable.

Take some yarn in the colour that is missing and a tapestry needle. Working from bottom to top and left to right, insert your needle from the wrong side of the knit to the right side at the bottom of the V of the stitch to be changed and draw your yarn under the two legs of the stitch lying above. Then, insert your needle at the bottom of the V again, at the point where you started.

Do the same thing for all the stitches that require duplicating. Make sure you leave a tail of sufficient length to allow you to weave it into the back of the knit.

Take some yarn in the colour that requires correcting and a tapestry needle.

The navy blue stitch should be sky blue.

Insert the needle at the base of the V, from wrong side to right.

Take the yarn over the right leg of the stitch and bring it back out at the top of the left leg.

Insert your yarn again at the base of the V.

You have duplicated the stitch.

Although the duplicated stitches technique works very well in terms of correcting errors, it also allows you to make some decorative additions to your knit. For example, you could embroider eyes, nose and cat's whiskers on the front of a child's sweater or on a knitted soft toy! Make sure that you work in the same size of yarn – it must be identical to the yarn you used for the colourwork.

Tip

These techniques mean you do not have to unravel your knit for a minor mistake. Note, however, that if you have too many stitches requiring correction on the same row you are better off unravelling it and knitting this part again.

CHAPTER 10

The steek technique

In knitting terms, a steek is a technique that is mainly used to turn sweaters knitted in the round into cardigans. It also enables you to make (depending on the pattern) openings at the neck and arms, or pockets on the front of a sweater.

What is steeking?

Steek is a Scottish word meaning to fasten or close. The idea is that you can adapt a knitted tube into a garment. Steeking is basically a process of cutting the knit. The noun 'steek' refers to the stitches knitted in the centre of the piece that will be cut to create the opening.

The process is simple: once the stitches have been secured, a straight vertical line is cut along a row of stitches in order to create an opening or to attach another piece to it. If the aim of steeking is to make a sweater into a cardigan, once you have cut your knit down the centre, the stitches are picked up to work the button bands, and finishing steps are needed to ensure the cut stitches do not unravel. Although button bands are the most common form of finishing, it is also possible to sew in a zip fastener.

This technique can be used for all knits but is more generally used for colourwork. But why would you knit colourwork in the round and then cut it open when you want to make a cardigan? Why not knit it in rows? Quite simply because colourwork is generally much more easily worked in the round: there are no purl rows and the rhythm/flow of work is more fluid. In addition, knitting in the round avoids the tension (gauge) differences that arise between a knit and purl row. Last but not least, it is often difficult to achieve neat edges when knitting colourwork in rows.

The best yarn for steeking

Advice before starting the steek

Make sure you have some small, very sharp scissors rather than ones with long blades. It is important to be able to snip little by little, so you are sure you are cutting in the right place. Once the work is cut, there is no going back!

Traditionally, woollen fibres are recommended for steeking. The advantage of these yarns, especially the ones that cannot be hand-washed (non-superwash) is that over time they can felt. This is exactly the effect that you want for a steek. Once secured, the stitches are cut, and with washing, the yarn will felt, adhere together, and ensure that the steek does not start to unravel. It is also possible (although not as advisable) to use this technique with machine washable wool (superwash). Note that in this case, the yarns will not felt and so it will be best to work the steek on the sewing machine (see opposite) rather than using the crochet method (see page 91) and to ensure that the cut edges are well secured inside using a ribbon hem finish.

Vegetable fibres (cotton, linen, silk) and synthetic fibres (acrylic, nylon) are not recommended for steeking, or indeed for knitting colourwork in general.

Steeking with a sewing machine or a crochet hook

The steeking process is much quicker on the sewing machine but of course this depends upon you having one available. Once the stitches have been secured and then cut, you need to apply seam tape to hold the yarn in place. The advantage of this method is that the inside looks aesthetically attractive and neatly finished.

If you use a crochet hook, you will need a hook of a smaller size than the knitting needles you used. This method takes longer than if you were using a sewing machine, but no other finishings are required once the stitches are crocheted together. However, the finished look on the inside is less aesthetically attractive than with the sewing machine method.

Now we will take a closer look at how these two steeking techniques are done.

Sewing machine method

To steek using the sewing machine, you simply need to follow the pattern instructions or decide, yourself, the place where you want to cut your knit.

When the steek consists of five central stitches, it is advisable to **cut in the centre of the third steek stitch** to ensure the opening is right in the centre. However, before you can cut it, you must secure the stitches by sewing two lines of stitches down either side. If you do not, the stitches of your knit will unravel one by one.

The first line of stitches should be between the second and third stitch of the steek, while the second line should be between the third and fourth.

Here are my recommendations to ensure your lines of stitches are successful:

+ You can choose either **straight stitch** or **zigzag** but the stitch size should be as small as possible. I prefer a straight stitch for a neat line. Once you have decided, work a line of stitches to either side of where the cut will be. This will ensure that the stitches of your knit are held firmly in place.

+ Use thread the same colour as your knit.

+ Sew the line of stitches on the **first side from bottom to top** and the line on the **second side from top to bottom**.

+ **Oversew** at the beginning and end so your seam cannot come undone.

+ **Take it slowly!** All the knitted stitches must be taken into the seam – you must not miss a single one. This is why I like to go back over the seam a second time to be on the safe side.

+ It is helpful to **stretch the stitches in your row apart** with your fingers to make sure you are sewing down the centre.

Once you have sewn the lines of stitches, it is time to start cutting! As my lines of machine stitches are at the centre of my second and third knitted stitches and at the centre of my third and fourth knitted stitches, and have now been secured, I can snip through the middle of the third knitted stitch.

You need to try to remain calm, don't stress, grab your scissors... and it's time to go! Once again, **it is essential to take it slowly.** Do not forget to **stretch the stitches apart with your fingers** to make sure you cut in the right place.

Depending on your pattern, some might advise picking up the stitches (using the working yarn to knit up the stitches along the edge) before embarking on the steek finishings, others advise after. Personally, I prefer picking up the stitches before.

As you can see in the photos above, you now have **a facing on the inside**, with the yarns unravelling up to the line of stitches (don't panic, this is normal!).

Here I have picked up my stitches while folding the facing to the inside. I have then knitted my button band in the normal way.

Additional advice

When the stitches down the edges are picked up, the colourwork tension (gauge) may change and the yarns may become a little too loose. If so, you can sew a small straight row of stitches (size 2.0) to stabilize the stitches on the right side, where they will be picked up. This trick gives you a neater finish.

Crochet method

This technique involves crocheting two lines of slip stitches on each side of the central stitch of the steek band, then you simply need to cut. The stitches are nicely secured and the bands fold inwards. It is worth considering using a contrasting colour for these crochet stitches so you are sure that you are cutting in the right place.

Here, on a steek of five central stitches, the principle will be similar to the seam. The crochet reinforcement on the left will use the left-hand strand of the third stitch and the right leg of the second stitch; the crochet reinforcement on the right will use the right leg of the third stitch and the left leg of the fourth stitch. The reinforcement will be worked row by row down the full length of the sweater and then the steek will be cut open down the centre of the third stitch.

Here are my recommendations for ensuring your crochet stitches are well secured.

+ The idea is to crochet the leg of the central stitch with the leg of the neighbouring stitch using slip stitch. To do so, use a **crochet hook that is smaller** than the size of your wool and a **contrasting yarn**, which should likewise be more lightweight than the one you used for your project.

+ You might find it easiest to **rotate your knit horizontally**. You can then work the steek from right to left.

+ Secure your yarn at the bottom of the work; it is often helpful to **fold your knit** so that the two stitches that you are crocheting together are more visible. Pass your hook through the two stitches, starting at the bottom, and work a stitch chain.

NOTE

If your colourwork comprises two colours on the same row, you can work a crocheted finish straight away.

If, however, your colourwork has three colours on the same row, you need to secure the stitches on the colourwork part using a sewing machine before working the crochet finish. This is what has been done on the Scafell cardigan in the tutorial before preparing the steek using the crochet method, because the crochet method cannot secure more than two colours at the same time.

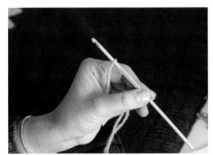

1. Start by tying a slip knot on the crochet needle.

2. Insert the hook under the two stitches of the sweater: under the right leg of the second stitch and the left leg of the third (central) stitch, along the row on the fold.

3. Wrap the yarn around the hook.

4. Pull the yarn through the loop on the hook: there are now two stitches on the hook.

5. Pull the second stitch through the first with the hook. You should only have a single stitch on your hook at the end.

6. Repeat in the same way on the next row: insert the hook under the two stitches of the sweater.

7. Wrap the yarn around the hook. Pull the hook back under the two stitches, bringing the yarn with it. Pull the hook through the stitch on the furthest right. Repeat to secure all the stitches in the row.

8. Cut the yarn and pull it through the last stitch. Repeat on the other side.

9. If you push the central stitch apart, you can see the contrasting yarn along the edges. Use sharply pointed scissors to cut through the centre of the third stitch.

10. Once you have finished cutting, pick up the stitches on each side on the row following the crochet line and knit the button bands.

Deciding which technique to use

In my opinion both techniques are equally valid and it is up to you to try them out and see which you prefer. The seam is certainly quicker on the machine, but you will need more time when it comes to the finishing (sewing in a seam band), while crocheting make take a bit longer but does not require any finishing. It will also depend on what you have available: a sewing machine or a crochet hook of the right size as well as the yarn that you used for your knit (rustic wool/superwash wool), or the number of colours on a single row.

Finishing the inside neatly

Working in the end of the yarn

You do not have to work in the ends of the yarn in the steek as you would for other yarns in the project, especially if your ends are all in the centre of the steek (start of the row), because they will subsequently be cut and protected by the finishings.

However, if you want, you can work the ends in one by one before cutting.

Sewing on a ribbon or bias binding

If you have used the sewing machine technique, once you have worked the button bands, the next stage is to **sew a ribbon to the inside to hide the internal facing**. This also allows you to protect your steek. You can singe the ends of the ribbon to stop them fraying. Simply cut to the same length as the sweater and sew on by hand with a matching thread. To do so, start at one corner and take your needle through a stitch of the knit, then through the ribbon. Skip a few stitches, then once again sew through one knitted stitch, then the ribbon. Repeat along the full length. Cut any tails of yarn that stick out from under the ribbon before sewing the other side, to ensure they will not show.

Over time, if the wool used is not machine-washable (so non-superwash), the facings will felt and the cut stitches will become one with the rest of the garment. This works with wool, but not with cotton, bamboo or acrylic, as these materials do not felt. Technically, however, your edges will be well protected by the ribbon.

Invisible seam

An invisible seam sewn with a tapestry needle is a good technique for securing your facings inside, if they are bothering you. It is particularly recommended if you have used the steek technique with a crochet hook and you want to finish the inside even more neatly.

Scallop stitch

Scallop stitch is another technique for attaching your facing inside and ensuring that it stays firmly attached. It takes longer and is more visible but ensures that the facing is held firmly in place.

An alternative finish:
the steek sandwich

If you are not keen on knitting the classic button bands and having to follow the finishing methods explained on the previous pages, you can use the steek sandwich method (a technique invented by Kate Davies). This technique is relatively simple and allows you to wrap your cut steek in two knitted bands, as if you are making a sandwich. Note, however, that it will add bulk and weight to your knit, so will not be appropriate for all projects.

Once your stitches are secured, and your band cut, pick up the stitches as you would for a classic button band on the right side of your work and knit four rows of stocking (stockinette) stitch, then leave your stitches waiting on the cable and needles.

On the wrong side of the knit, with a second pair of needles, pick up (but without knitting) the loops formed by the first row of picked-up stitches (worked on the right side). Knit three rows of stocking (stockinette) stitch, starting with a row of knit stitch.

You now have two knitted bands that you will need to attach together to enclose the steek. To do so, with the right side of the knit towards you, take a third needle and use the three-needle cast-off method without casting off the stitches: knit a stitch from the band on the right side with the equivalent stitch on the band on the wrong side, continuing in the same way right along the opening. You now have a single row of stitches and your steek is enclosed in the sandwich. Work i-cord edging, inserting buttonholes if required.

i-cord cast-off: cast on 3 extra sts onto your work, k2, k2tog tbl. You now have 3 sts on the right needle. Transfer them back to the left needle and do the same again: k2, k2tog tbl. Transfer them back to the left needle and carry on. When you have 3 sts left, k2tog, k1, place the sts back on the left needle. k2tog tbl. Cut the yarn, thread it through the last stitch and pull to secure.

Right side.

Wrong side.

TO BLOCK BEFORE OR AFTER CUTTING THE STEEK?

It is not advisable to block your knit fully before cutting the steek: your yarn may unravel and come out of the crocheted or machine-sewn reinforcement.

You can, however, block the front and back lightly with steam if you want, but note that the full blocking process should be done right at the end of the project, once the steek has been cut and the button band knitted.

Adding a steek to a sweater pattern

If your pattern does not include steeking, that is, it is designed just in sweater form, but you want to make it into a cardigan, it is possible to add the steek yourself.

When you start knitting, whether at the top or bottom, add five additional stitches and use stitch markers to indicate clearly where the steek begins and ends. These five central stitches will not be part of the total number of stitches on the pattern and will be knitted in stocking (stockinette) stitch throughout. This means that they will be worked in simple stocking (stockinette) stitch when you are knitting the ribbing around the neck and the bottom of the body and they will not have the motif on the colourwork section. It is still important, however, to knit some coloured stitches into the steek of the colourwork part so the yarn is carried over the back. This will avoid being left with long floats, which would then be cut.

You might also consider starting your row at the centre of your steek to avoiding working in all the colourwork yarn tails at the end. They will be cut then protected by the crochet finishing, or the facing sewn on if you are using the sewing machine method. In this case, work the colour that you are finishing as far as the centre and start again in the new colour likewise in the centre so that all the yarns arrive at the same place – the middle of the steek.

If you are knitting in colourwork that features a **series of small motifs**, the position of the steek in relation to the motif is not particularly important. You can therefore rely on the pattern chart. **On the other hand, you do need to take care with bigger motifs**: if your colourwork comprises large motifs, it is important to look at how they will be positioned on either side of the steek (and subsequently the button band). You may need to redesign the motif so the separation differs from the one shown on the pattern.

Let us take the example of a snowflake motif (a traditional Scandinavian colourwork design), shown on your pattern in two parts: you will need to redesign it as a full motif for a steeked version. This will allow the motif to appear in full on either side of your button band and not cut in half. The number of times the motif is repeated will be identical but the motif will be divided differently.

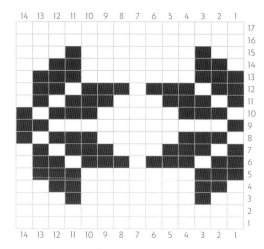

Original design of the sweater pattern.

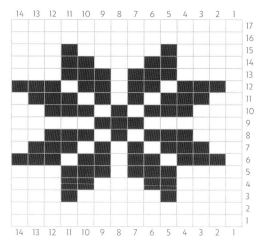

Snowflake redesigned so it is well positioned after steeking.

CHAPTER 11

Finishing your knitting

Once you have finished knitting, there are still a few stages before your work is complete. This finishing is essential, especially with colourwork.

Working in the end of the yarn

When you turn your knit inside out, you will see a number of tails of yarn where you introduced a new colour. There are several methods of properly finishing your knit.

Work out in which direction the tails should be worked in

When you need to work in two neighbouring tails, cross them so that a hole does not form in the centre. Then work in the strands in opposite directions to ensure the hole is closed up. You can pull gently on the yarn of the first stitch to tighten it and make it secure. Repeat for all your tails of yarn.

Once your tails of yarn are properly positioned, use a tapestry needle to work them all in.

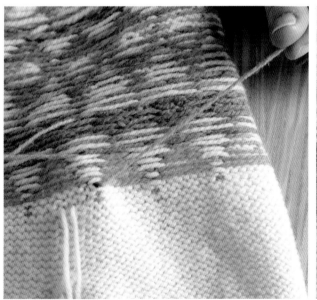

The tails of yarn pulled in this direction form a hole, so you need to pull them in the opposite direction.

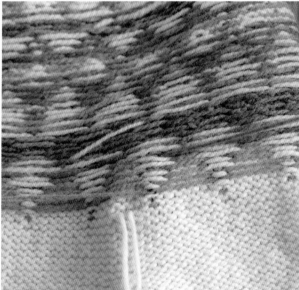

The yarns close up the holes created previously, so they must be worked in this direction.

Working in the tails of yarn

Using your tapestry needle, weave in the yarn from top to bottom for about 2.5cm (1in) in the direction the yarn would have gone had it been knitted and not cut. Make sure you do not pull it too tightly.

Tying the tails of yarn together

You do not have to weave in the tails one by one, you can also tie them off in pairs. This technique is common and you can even see it on some traditional knits. You should note, however, that with this method, as the wool can felt, the knotted strands have a tendency to bind together during washing, which will not be the case with superwash wool. I have tried out this method and found it to work very well.

Tip

For colourwork with numerous colour changes, such as Fair Isle, it is possible to work in your tails of yarn as you knit.

Blocking your knitting

Difference between a blocked sleeve (left) and a non-blocked sleeve (right): before blocking the knit is uneven and bumpy, even with good tension (gauge). After blocking, the knit is flat and the colourwork stands out.

Your colourwork knit is not finished until it has been blocked. This is trumpeted by all colourwork knitters, regardless of where they are from. Blocking is absolutely indispensable at the end of any knitting project, but is even more the case with colourwork, if you want to achieve a good finish. It allows you to ensure that the final measurements of your knit are correct, but also to smooth out the colourwork sections and resolve any tension (gauge) problems.

Here are the different stages of successfully blocking your colourwork knit:

Washing

Fill a basin with fresh, lukewarm water (hot water could cause your knit to felt) and add a small amount of detergent. It doesn't matter whether you opt for no-rinse or rinse-out detergents (see Chapter 2, page 23).

Then simply immerse your knit gently in the water, without rubbing. Make sure your knit is fully submerged and check that all parts are saturated. Press down gently on any areas that are not yet soaked. When no more bubbles rise to the surface, this means that your knitwear is completely soaked in the soapy water. Leave to soak without touching for 20 to 30 minutes.

If you are using a rinse-out detergent, you will need to change the water and soak the knitwear in clean water for 15 to 30 minutes.

Tip

If your work comprises several very different colours, such as white/beige and navy blue, for example, it is best to block using cold water so there is less risk of the colour running. You can also add a colour catcher sheet to the water.

Getting the moisture out

Now it's time to get the water out. Remove your knit gently from the water – under no circumstances be tempted to try to wring it out. Instead, squeeze gently, then prepare a large towel. Make sure your knit is well supported so it does not stretch. Wrap your knit in the towel to form a sausage. Then put it on the ground and press with your feet by walking along it.

If you have used superwash wool, you can put the knit in a pillowcase or laundry net and put it in the washing machine to spin. If you choose this option, set it on a moderate speed and ensure that your wool can go into the machine in the first place.

Blocking

Once the knit is well wrung out, you can lay it out flat on a mat. The next step is very important for colourwork: you need to pin your work to the shape and measurements given in the pattern. You can use blocking pins, but I find blocking combs are even more effective.

Stretch the colourwork part of your knit slightly to smooth it out.

The blocked knit will remember the shape you give it. You won't need to repeat this process and in future you can just wash it normally. For socks, sock blockers are available, which are very handy.

NOTE

It is perfectly possible to block the circular yoke of your colourwork before you knit the rest of the sweater, whether to check your tension (gauge) or to motivate you to get on with the rest. In this case, knit the whole yoke and suspend the stitches on a long piece of yarn. Leave it to soak and gently squeeze out any excess moisture. You can then pin it out very delicately, being sure not to tug at it: it is difficult to know what form it will take before you have knitted the body, so it is important not to pull it out of shape.

Washing wool on a day-to-day basis

There are two techniques for washing wool.

+ The first consists of always hand-washing and leaving your knitwear to soak for a while in a basin of lukewarm water with your preferred laundry detergent (see Chapter 2, page 23). For getting the moisture out, follow the instructions given on page 103 (towel or washing machine).

   If you have knitted your colourwork project with a natural, rustic, non-superwash wool, there is a risk that it will felt if you put it in the machine. So, only wash your knitted fabric by hand in lukewarm water.

Tip

Before putting your knit into the washing machine, check that the wool you have used is definitely machine washable. It cannot be stressed enough that while superwash wools can go through the machine, none of the others can.

+ The second consists of machine washing. Warning: I strongly advise you to wash your swatch in the machine first to see how it reacts before you wash your sweater, cardigan or other item. Personally, I either use the 30°C (86°F) programme for delicates, or the woollens programme. In terms of spinning, I would recommend setting the spin cycle to 800–1,000 rpm: it needs to be quite fast to hold your garment against the wall of the machine and prevent it from moving about in the drum and getting damaged. Friction is the basic cause of felting (as the weave shrinks, it loses its flexibility and hardens into felt).

Additional tips for machine washing

+ Use a gentle laundry detergent.

+ Wash in cold or lukewarm water depending on the knit. Hot water can cause woollen garments to shrink.

+ Wash your treasured knits individually.

+ Turn your garments inside out before washing.

+ Select the shortest wash time for woollens and crease-proof items.

+ Do not use a tumble-dryer. As with hot water, hot air can cause woollen garments to shrink.

+ Do not wring your knits out. It is better to wrap them in a towel and dry them flat on a second dry towel.

Storing knitwear

Here are a few tips to ensure the longevity of your knitwear.

+ It is better to fold knitwear than hang it.

+ Do not store dirty sweaters in your wardrobe: they may attract moths, but in addition, stains may become permanent.

+ To ward off moths, put cedar balls or shavings, or lavender sachets in your wardrobes. Cedar shavings can also absorb excess moisture, which prevents mould. Wrap them in cloth to prevent them from staining your knitwear.

+ Do not store your knitwear in an airtight container. Natural fibres, which are often used in colourwork, need to breathe. A canvas or muslin bag is a better option.

Removing fuzz

I always use a battery-operated (or electric) wool shaver, which is a great tool for removing fuzz and bobbles. It only has one speed and you simply run it gently over the sweater. Do not use it on lace as it may tear the lace, but it works very well on colourwork knits. I find it particularly useful for projects in DK (8-ply/light worsted), 5-ply (sport) or 4-ply (fingering).

The Gleener is another hand tool for removing fuzz and bobbles. Simply spread out the garment on a hard surface and run it from top to bottom. My recommendation would be to test the blade in the least visible area of the garment first, for example, an inside seam. I also have one that I use for big Aran (worsted) colourwork winter jumpers.

The patterns

Blisco hat

The Blisco hat is a very accessible pattern that is ideal for colourwork beginners: it has only two colours per row and you rarely need to strand the yarn across the back. It is given in three sizes so it can be knitted for all ages. It would be fun to knit a range for the whole family.

YOU WILL NEED

+ **DK (8-ply/light worsted) wool**
  · Main colour (MC):
  95/115/125m (104/126/137yd)

  · Contrasting colour (CC):
  60/90/100m (66/98/109yd)

+ Circular needles 3.75mm
  (UK 9, US 5), cable 40–60cm
  (16–24in)

+ Circular needles 3.5mm
  (UK 9/10, US 4), for the
  ribbing, cable 40–60cm
  (16–24in)

+ Place marker

+ Tapestry needle

+ A pompom

SIZES

Size: child / adult 1 / adult 2
Circumference of finished hat: 42/48/55cm (16½/19/21¾in)
Head circumference (after blocking, without stretching): 46–50/51–55/56–60cm
(18–19¾/20–21¾/22–23½in)
Hat height: 19/20/22cm (7½/7¾/8¾in)

SWATCH 10 × 10CM (4 × 4IN)

23 stitches × 30 rows stocking (stockinette) stitch in the round using 3.75mm
(UK 9, US 5) needles (or another size depending on your swatch)

Yarns used, from bottom to top:
Athéna by Lain'amourée, colours
Baisers de groseilles and Les pieds
dans le sable; colours Aime comme
mademoiselle and Naturel; colours
Les pieds dans le sable and Noël sous
les pins.

Instructions

Ribbing

Using 3.5mm (UK 9/10, US 4) needles, cast on 96/112/128 sts using the continental, long-tail cast-on method. Join in the round and PM (place marker) to denote beg of round.

Work in 2×2 rib across 10/11/12cm (4/4¼/4¾in).

Crown of hat

Swap to 3.75mm (UK 9, US 5) needles and work the colourwork following the chart below. Rep the motif right across the round.
Cont until chart is complete, then knit until hat measures 24/25.5/28cm (9½/10/11in) in total.

NOTE

To respect colour dominance, use CC as the dominant colour and MC as the non-dominant colour. At round 14, swap dominance, holding MC as the dominant colour and CC as the non-dominant colour.

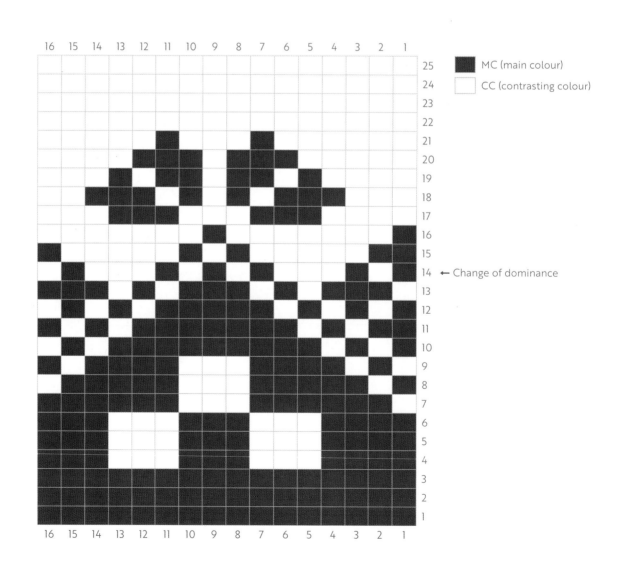

■ MC (main colour)

☐ CC (contrasting colour)

← Change of dominance

Crown decreases

For size adult 2 **only**
k14, k2tog, rep from * to * to end of round.
k13, k2tog, rep from * to * to end of round.

For sizes adult 1 **and** adult 2 **only**
k12, k2tog, rep from * to * to end of round.
k11, k2tog rep from * to * to end of round.

For all sizes
k10, k2tog rep from * to * to end of round.

k9, k2tog rep from * to * to end of round.

k8, k2tog rep from * to * to end of round.

k7, k2tog rep from * to * to end of round.

k6, k2tog rep from * to * to end of round.

k5, k2tog rep from * to * to end of round.

k4, k2tog rep from * to * to end of round.

k3, k2tog rep from * to * to end of round.

k2, k2tog rep from * to * to end of round.

k1, k2tog rep from * to * to end of round.

k2tog rep from * to * to end of round.

Cut yarn leaving a tail of around 30cm (11¾in).
Thread through remaining sts and pull yarn
tightly to close hole.

Finishing

Weave in ends with a tapestry needle. Block
the hat to highlight the colourwork by placing
on a blocking mat or a head-shaped object
such as a balloon. Add a pompom and fold the
ribbing up on itself.

Helvellyn sweater

The Helvellyn is a unisex sweater for a baby or child. It makes a perfect first colourwork project. It does not require you to strand your yarn behind and there are never more than two colours per round. In addition, as the colourwork is all in the border at the bottom of the sweater, you will not have to manage your tension (gauge) at the same time as working decreases or increases. This pattern is knitted from the top down.

YOU WILL NEED

+ **DK (8-ply/light worsted) wool**
  · Main colour (MC):
  230/(280:320:360)/(400:450:500:550)/(650:750)m
  [252/(306:350:394)/(437:492:547:601)/(711:820)yd]

  · Contrasting colour (CC):
  15/(15:20:20)/(20:25:25:30)/(35:35)m
  [16/(16:22:22)/(22:27:27:33)/(38:38)yd]

+ Circular needles 3.75mm (UK 9, US 5), for the body and the sleeves, cable 60–80cm (24–32in)

+ Circular needles 3.5mm (UK 9/10, US 4), for the ribbing, cable 60–80cm (24–32in)

+ Stitch markers

+ Pieces of yarn for stitch holders

+ Tapestry needle

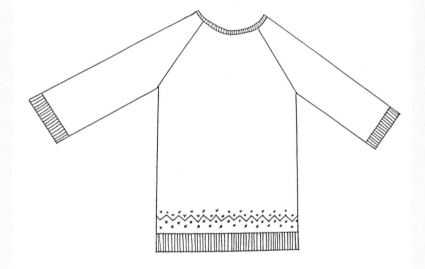

SIZES

3/(6:12:18) months/(2:4:6:8)years/(10:12) years

SWATCH 10 × 10CM (4 × 4IN)

23 stitches × 30 rows stocking (stockinette) stitch in the round using 3.75mm (UK 9, US 5) needles (or another size depending on your swatch)

Yarns used: Einband by Istex Lópi
(4-ply [fingering] knitted double-
stranded), colours navy (0118) and
white (0851). Pink version (see
page 34): Athéna DK by Lain'amourée,
colours Les pieds dans le sable and
Baisers de groseilles.

Instructions

Yoke

Using 3.5mm (UK 9/10, US 4) needles, cast on 66/(72:72:82)/(86:88:88:90)/(92:94) sts using long-tall cast-on method. Join the sts in the round and PM to denote beg of round.

Work 5 rounds of 1×1 rib.

Swap to 3.75mm (UK 9, US 5) needles and knit 1 round, placing markers as follows:

k9/(11:12:13)/(14:15:16:16)/(17:17) sts for the back, PM, k1, PM, k12/(12:10:13)/(12:12:10:10)/(10:10) sts for the sleeve, PM, k1, PM, k19/(22:24:26)/(29:30:32:33)/(34:35) sts for the front, PM, k1, PM, k12/(12:10:13)/(12:12:10:10)/(10:10) sts for the sleeve, PM, k1, PM, k10/(11:12:13)/(15:15:16:17)/(17:18) sts for the back, PM for start of row.

Next round: start raglan increases, to be worked every other row.

Round 1: k to first marker, *M1R, sm, k1 (raglan), sm, M1L, k to next marker*; rep from * to * three more times, k to end of round.

Each inc round creates 8 additional sts.

Round 2: knit.

Rep these 2 rounds until you have 13/(13:15:15)/(16:17:19:20)/(21:22) rounds of raglan increases from start, ending on a round 2. You now have 170 / (176:192:202) / (214:224:240:250)/(260:270) sts on your needles, distributed as follows: 38/(38:40:43)/(44:46:48:50)/(52:54) sts for each sleeve, 45/(48:54:56)/(61:64:70:73)/(76:79) sts for the front, 45/(48:54:56)/(61:64:70:73)/(76:79) sts for the back and 4 raglan sts between the markers.

Separating the sleeves and the body

Divide for sleeves: knit to marker, remove marker, k1 (raglan), remove marker, hold 38/(38:40:43)/(44:46:48:50)/(52:54) sts for right sleeve, cast on 2/(2:2:3)/(3:3:3:3)/(3:3) sts for armhole and place new marker for start of round, cast on 2/(2:2:2)/(3:3:3:3)/(3:3) sts, remove marker, k1 (raglan), remove marker, k45/(48:54:56)/(61:64:70:73)/(76:79) for the front, remove marker, k1 (raglan), remove marker, hold 38/(38:40:43)/(44:46:48:50)/(52:54) sts for left sleeve, cast on 4/(4:4:5)/(6:6:6:6)/(6:6) sts, remove marker, k1 (raglan), remove marker, knit to former start-of-round marker and remove it. Your start-of-round will now be under the armhole.

The raglan sts are now located in front and back sections: 2 raglan sts are added to the back count and the other 2 raglan sts are added to the front count of the sweater. They are no longer denoted by the markers.

Body

You now have 102/(108:120:126)/(138:144:156:162)/(168:174) sts on your needles for the body.

Continue to knit in st st until body measures 6.5/(7:9.5:11.5)/(16:18:21:25)/(27:29)cm [2½/(2¾:3¾:4½)/(6¼:7:8¼:9¾)/(10¾:11½)in] from under the armhole.

Start knitting the colourwork section, following the chart. The chart shows a sequence of 12 sts to make it easier to read, but in reality, it is a rep pattern of 6 sts.

To respect colour dominance, hold the dominant colour (the contrasting colour, in this case white) in the left hand and the non-dominant colour (the main colour, in this case blue) in your right hand if you are knitting in the continental style.

Cut the contrasting colour yarn and, using only the main colour, knit 2 rounds.

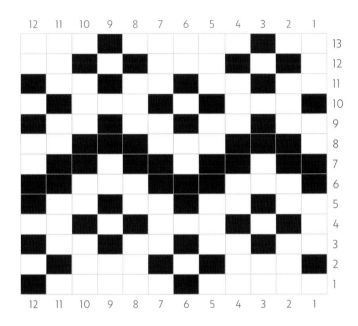

☐ MC (main colour)

■ CC (contrasting colour)

> **NOTE**
>
> If your tension (gauge) is too tight when knitting the colourwork, I recommend using needles one size bigger to work this section.

Swap to 3.5mm (UK 9/10, US 4) needles. Work 2 / (2:2.5:2.5) / (3:3:3:3) / (3:3)cm [¾ / (¾:1:1) / (1¼:1¼:1¼:1¼) / (1¼:1¼)in] of 1×1 rib stitch. Cast off loosely.

Sleeves

Using 3.75mm (UK 9, US 5) needles, place the 38 / (38:40:43) / (44:46:48:50) / (52:54) sts of the sleeve on your needles.

Trick

When you pick up the stitches under the arms, a hole can form between the suspended stitches and the stitches picked up from either side of the armhole. There are a couple of methods of resolving this problem:

+ you can sew up the hole using the ends of the yarn at the end of the project;

+ or you can pick up 2 or 4 additional stitches and work the decrease round so that you get down to the number of stitches given in the pattern (see 'Decrease round', overleaf). I recommend this method.

PM to denote the beginning of the round.

Starting from the middle of the armhole, pick up 2/(2:2:2)/(3:3:3:3)/(3:3) sts from the centre towards the side (from right to left). Knit the 38/(38:40:43)/(44:46:48:50)/(52:54) sts of the sleeve then pick up 2/(2:2:3)/(3:3:3:3)/(3:3) sts for the level of the armhole.

You now have 42/(42:44:48)/(50:52:54:56)/(58:60) sts on your needles.

Knit 2 rounds.

Decrease round: k1, k2tog, knit to third stitch from end of row, ssk, k1 (= 2 decreases).

Rep decrease round 3/(3:3:4)/(4:5:5:5)/(6:6) more times every 3/(3.5:3.5:3.5)/(3.5:3.5:4:5)/(5:5)cm [1¼/(13/8:13/8:13/8)/(13/8:13/8:1½:2)/(2:2) in] while continuing to knit 1 round of st st between each decrease round.

You now have 34/(34:36:38)/(40:40:42:44)/(44:46) sts on your needles.

Continue in st st until the sleeve measures 12/(14:17:17.5)/(20:23.5:26:31)/(35:37)cm [4½/(5½:6½:6¾)/(8:9¼:10½:12½)/(14:14½)in] in length from the armhole.

Swap to the smaller needles and work 2/(2:2.5:2.5)/(3:3:3:3)/(3:3)cm [1¼/(¾/(¾:1:1)/(1¼:1¼:1¼:1¼)/(1¼:1¼)in] in 1×1 rib. Cast off loosely (see Further information, page 137).

Rep for the second sleeve.

Finishing

Weave in ends with a tapestry needle. Close up the holes under the arms with a few sts if needed. Block the sweater to adjust it to the final dimensions and highlight the colourwork.

Helvellyn final measurements

Note: the measurements given are approximate and very much depend on the swatch.

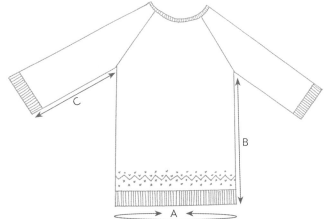

SIZE	A Around chest	B Body length from bottom of armhole	C Sleeve length from bottom of armhole
3 MONTHS	44.5cm (17½in)	13.5cm (5¼in)	16cm (6¼in)
6 MONTHS	47cm (18½in)	14cm (5½in)	18cm (7in)
12 MONTHS	52cm (20½in)	17cm (6¾in)	20.5cm (8in)
18 MONTHS	55cm (21½in)	19cm (7½in)	21cm (8¼in)
2 YEARS	60cm (23½in)	24cm (9½in)	23cm (9in)
4 YEARS	62.5cm (24½in)	26cm (10½in)	26.5cm (10½in)
6 YEARS	68cm (26¾in)	29cm (11½in)	29cm (11½in)
8 YEARS	70.5cm (27¾in)	33cm (13in)	34cm (13½in)
10 YEARS	73cm (28¾in)	35cm (14in)	38cm (15in)
12 YEARS	76cm (30in)	37cm (14½in)	40cm (16in)

Bowfell sweater

Bowfell is a women's sweater that is at a beginner's level in terms of colourwork but will still be of interest to more experienced knitters. It does not require you to strand your yarn behind and there are never more than two colours per round. It is the perfect pattern for anyone who wants to start on colourwork with an adult project.

YOU WILL NEED

+ **5-ply (sport) yarn**
  · Main colour (MC):
  980:1,030/(1,150:
  1,200:1,250)/(1,300:
  1,350:1,400)m
  [1,072:1,126/(1,258:
  1,312:1,367)/(1,422:
  1,476:1,531)yd]

  · Contrasting colour (CC):
  100:100/(120:120:
  150)/(150:150:150)m
  [109:109/(131:131:
  164)/(164:164:164)yd]

+ 3.5mm (UK 9/10, US 4) circular needles for the ribbing, cable 80cm (31½in)

+ 3.75mm (UK 9, US 5) circular needles for the body and sleeves, cable 80cm (31½in)

+ 4mm (UK 8, US 6) circular needles for the colourwork (optional: only if your tension/gauge is a lot tighter when you are knitting colourwork), cable 80cm (31½in)

+ Stitch markers

+ Waste yarn for stitch holders

+ Tapestry needle

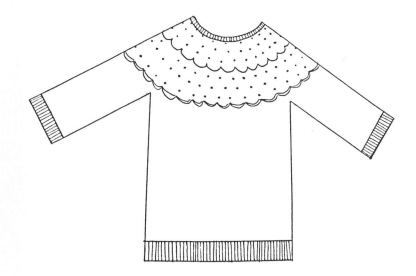

SIZES

85:92/(98:105:110)/(115:122:128)cm
[33½:36¼/(38½:41¼:43¾)/(45¼:48:50½)in] around the bust (finished garment measurements)
0 to 10cm (4in) of positive ease recommended

SWATCH 10 × 10CM (4 × 4IN)

24 stitches × 34 rows stocking (stockinette) stitch in the round using 3.75mm (UK 9, US 5) needles (or another size depending on your swatch)

Instructions

Yoke

Using 3.5mm (UK 9/10, US 4) needles and the contrasting colour (CC), cast on 96:100/(108:112:120)/(124:128:128) sts using the long-tail cast-on method. Join the sts in the round and PM to denote beg of round (which will always be between the back and the left sleeve).

Work in 2×2 rib across 5 rounds.

Next round: swap to 3.75mm (UK 9, US 5) needles and knit 1 round.

Knit 1 additional round, increasing 14:15/(17:18:15)/(16:17:22) sts distributed equally across round (I recommend using M1L, which are the least visible, see Further information, page 136).

You now have 110:115/(125:130:135)/(140:145:150) sts on your needles.

Knit 0:2/(3:5:5)/(5:5:5) rounds.

Follow the colourwork chart for your size, either continuing with 3.75mm (UK 9, US 5) needles or swapping to 4mm (UK 8, US 6) needles (only if you knit colourwork with a tighter tension): rep the 14 sts of the chart across the round. You should have 22:23/(25:26:27)/(28:29:30) repetitions of the motif per round.

> **NOTE**
>
> When you work an increase in the chart in the form of an M1L or M1R (see Further information, page 136), always pick up the yarn between stitches, not the yarn stranded behind, then work the new stitch with this same colour.

Here is the stitch count for each round of increases on the chart:

	Sizes 85–105cm (33½–41¼in)	Sizes 110–128cm (43¼–50½in)
Round 3:	176:184/(200:208)	(216)/(224:232:240)
Round 13:	242:253/(275:286)	(297)/(308:319:330)
Round 16:	264:276/(300:312)	(324)/(336:348:360)
Round 36:	308:322/(350:364)	(378)/(392:406:420)

Now the colourwork is complete, you have 308:322/(350:364:378)/(392:406:420) sts on your needles.

Using the 3.75mm (UK 9, US 5) needles, knit 1 round, placing two markers, which will denote the arms, as follows: k154:161/(175:182:189)/(196:203:210) sts, PM, k94:100/(108:116:120)/(126:134:142) sts, PM. Knit to end of round.

German short rows (GSR)

1. Knit to 5 sts after marker 1, turn work so WS is facing and work a GSR (see Further information, page 136).

2. Purl to 5 sts after marker 2, turn work so RS is facing, bring yarn to front and work a GSR.

3. Knit to 5 sts before preceding GSR, turn work so WS is facing and work a GSR.

4. Purl to 5 sts before preceding GSR, turn work so RS is facing, bring yarn to front and work a GSR.

5. Knit to 5 sts before preceding GSR, turn work so WS is facing and work a GSR.

6. Purl to 5 sts before preceding GSR, turn work so RS is facing, bring yarn to front and work a GSR.

Yarns used: Ulysse by De Rerum Natura, colours Sel and Lagon (size 85 knitted with 5cm [2in] of positive ease).

⑦ Knit to 5 sts before preceding GSR, turn work so WS is facing and work a GSR.

⑧ Purl to 5 sts before preceding GSR, turn work so RS is facing, bring yarn to front and work a GSR.

⑨ Knit to start-of-round marker.

⑩ Knit one additional round, working the double-stranded sts (those formed by the GSRs) as a single stitch and removing marker 1 and marker 2.

Knit 1:1/(4:6:3)/(6:8:8) row(s).

Separating the sleeves and the body

Divide for sleeves:
k94:100/(108:116:120)/(126:134:142) sts for the back, hold 60:61/(67:66:69)/ (70:69:68) sts for the sleeve, cast on 8:10/ (10:10:12)/(12:12:12) sts under the armhole, k94:100/(108:116:120)/(126:134:142) sts for the front, suspend 60:61/(67:66:69)/ (70:69:68) sts for the sleeve, cast on 8:10/(10:10:12)/(12:12:12) sts under the armhole.

Body

You now have 204:220/(236:252:264)/ (276:292:308) sts on your needles for the body.

Continue to knit in st st until body measures 33:34/(34:35:35)/(35:37:37)cm [13:13½/(13½:13¾:13¾)/(13¾:14½:14½)in] from under armhole, or 5cm (2in) less than desired length.

Swap to 3.5mm (UK 9/10, US 4) needles and work 5cm (2in) in 2×2 rib. Cast off loosely (see Further information, page 137).

Sleeves

Using 3.75mm (UK 9, US 5) needles, place the 60:61/(67:66:69)/(70:69:68) sts of the sleeve on your needles.

PM to denote the beginning of the round and, starting from the middle of the armhole, pick up 4:5/(5:5:6)/(6:6:6) sts from the centre towards the edge (from right to left). Knit the 60:61/(67:66:69)/(70:69:68) sts of the sleeve then pick up 4:5/(5:5:6)/(6:6:6) sts from the armhole.

You now have 68:71/(77:76:81)/(82:81:80) sts on your needles.

Decrease round: k1, k2tog, knit to last 3 sts from end of round, ssk, k1 (= 2 decreases).

Rep this decrease round 9:10/(11:11:13)/ (12:11:11) more times, every 3.5:3/(3:3:2.5)/ (2.5:3:3)cm [1½:1¼/(1¼:1¼:1)/(1:1¼:1¼)in].

For sizes 92, 98, 110 and 122cm (36¼,38½, 43¼ and 48in), knit 1 round with a single decrease as follows: k1, k2tog, knit to end of round.

You now have 48:48/(52:52:52)/(56:56:56) sts on your needles.

Trick

When you pick up the stitches under the arms, a hole can form between the held stitches and the stitches picked up from either side of the armhole. There are a couple of methods of resolving this problem:

+ you can sew up the hole using the ends of the yarn at the end of the project;

+ or you can pick up 2 or 4 additional stitches and work the decrease round until you get down to the number of stitches given in the pattern (see 'Decrease round', above). I recommend this method.

Continue to knit in st st until the sleeve measures 37cm (14½in), or 10cm (4in) less than the required length: the total length of the sleeve in the pattern is 47cm (18½in). The ribbed cuffs will then be folded back to achieve a length of 42cm (16½in).

Swap to 3.5mm (UK 9/10, US 4) needles and work 10cm (4in) in 2×2 rib. Cast off your sts. Rep for the second sleeve.

Finishing

Weave in ends with a tapestry needle. Block the sweater to smooth out the colourwork and adjust it to the final dimensions. Fold up the ribbed cuffs.

Colourwork charts

	CC (contrasting colour)		CC increase
	MC (main colour)		MC increase
			No stitch

Sizes 85–105cm (33½–41¼in)

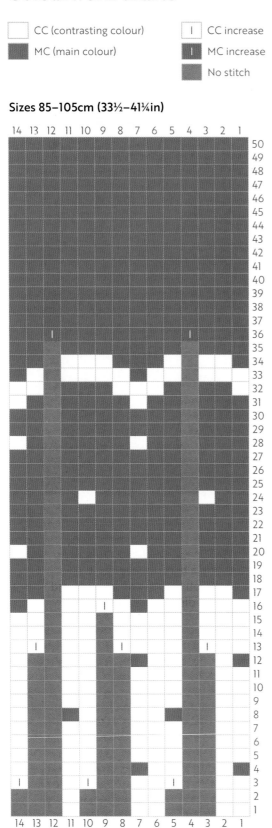

Sizes 110–128cm (43¼–50½in)

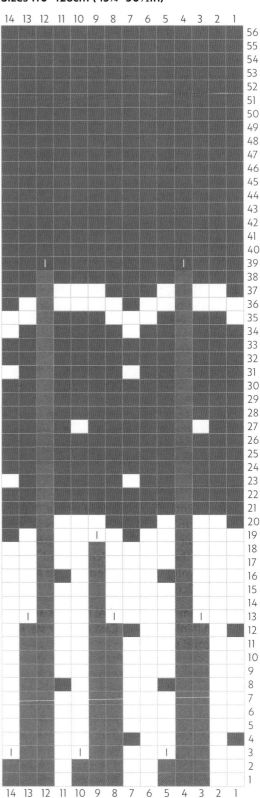

Bowfell final measurements

Note that the measurements given are approximate and very much depend on the swatch.

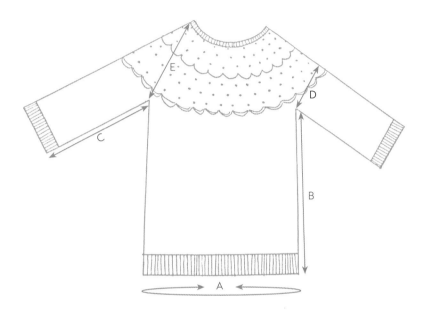

SIZE (cm)	A Around chest	B Body length from bottom of armhole	C Sleeve length from bottom of armhole	D Sleeve width	E Depth of yoke (edges included)
85	85cm (33½in)	38cm (15in)	42cm (16½in)	28.5cm (11¼in)	21cm (8¼in)
92	92cm (36¼in)	39cm (15½in)	42cm (16½in)	29.5cm (11¾in)	22cm (8¾in)
98	98.5cm (38¾in)	39cm (15½in)	42cm (16½in)	32cm (12½in)	23cm (9in)
105	105cm (41¼in)	40cm (16in)	42cm (16½in)	32cm (12½in)	24cm (9½in)
110	110cm (43¼in)	40cm (16in)	42cm (16½in)	34cm (13½in)	25cm (9¾in)
115	115cm (45¼in)	40cm (16in)	42cm (16½in)	34cm (13½in)	26cm (10½in)
122	122cm (48in)	42cm (16½in)	42cm (16½in)	34cm (13½in)	26.5cm (10½in)
128	128.5cm (50½in)	42cm (16½in)	42cm (16½in)	34cm (13½in)	26.5cm (10½in)

Scafell sweater

While this women's sweater does not require the yarn to be stranded across the back, several rounds are knitted with three yarns at the same time. You therefore need to be comfortable with colourwork technique before attempting this project. This sweater has a large circular, colourwork yoke, a straight body and long ribbing at the cuffs and at the bottom of the body.

YOU WILL NEED

+ **5-ply (sport) yarn**
  · Main colour (MC): 860:940/(1,050: 1,140:1,280)/(1,365: 1,400:1,440)m [941:1,028/(1,148: 1,247:1,400)/(1,493: 1,531:1,575)yd]

  · Contrasting colours 1 and 2 (CC1 and CC2): 150m (164yd) for each contrasting colour

+ 3.5mm (UK 9/10, US 4) circular needles, for the ribbing, cable 80cm (31½in)

+ 3.75mm (UK 9, US 5) circular needles, for the body and sleeves, cable 80cm (31½in)

+ 4mm (UK 8, US 6) circular needles, for the colourwork (optional: only if your tension/gauge is a lot tighter when you are knitting colourwork), cable 80cm (31½in)

+ Stitch markers

+ Waste yarn for stitch holders

+ Tapestry needle

SIZES

85:92/(98:105:110)/(116:123:129)cm [33½:36¼/(38½:41¼:43¾)/(45½:48½:50¾)in] around the bust (finished garment measurements)
0 to 10cm (4in) of positive ease recommended

SWATCH 10 × 10CM (4 × 4IN)

24 stitches × 34 rows stocking (stockinette) stitch in the round using 3.75mm (UK 9, US 5) needles (or another size depending on your swatch)

Yarns used: Ulysse by De Rerum Natura, colours Sel, Argile and Doré (size 85cm/33½in, knitted with 5cm (2in) positive ease).

Instructions

Ribbing

Using 3.5mm (UK 9/10, US 4) needles and the main colour (MC), cast on 92:100/(108:112:120)/(124:128:128) sts, using the long-tail cast-on method. Join the sts in the round and PM to denote beg of round (which will always be between the back and the left sleeve).

Work five rounds in 2×2 rib.

Next round: swap to 3.75mm (UK 9, US 5) needles and knit 1 round.

Knit 1 additional round, increasing 3:0/(2:3:0)/(1:2:7) sts distributed equally across the round (I recommend using M1L, which are the least visible, see Further information, page 136).

You now have 95:100/(110:115:120)/(125:130:135) sts on your needles.

Knit. 0:0/(1:2:2)/(4:4:4) round(s).

Follow the colourwork chart for your size, either continuing with 3.75mm (UK 9, US 5) needles or swapping to 4mm (UK 8, US 6) needles (only if you knit colourwork with a tighter tension/gauge): rep the 16 sts of the chart across the round. You should have 19:20/(22:23:24)/(25:26:27) repetitions of the motif per round.

> **NOTE**
>
> When you work an increase in the chart in the form of M1L or M1R (see Further information, page 136), always pick up the yarn of the MC to work the increase and not that of the CC, then knit the new st with this same colour.

Here is the stitch count for each round of increases on the chart:

Sizes 85–105cm (33½–41¼in)

Round 2: 152:160/(176:184)

Round 6: 190:200/(220:230)

Round 9: 228:240/(264:276)

Round 19: 266:280/(308:322)

Round 25: 304:320/(352:368)

Sizes 110–129cm (43¼–50¾in)

Round 3: (192)/(200:208:216)

Round 8: (240)/(250:260:270)

Round 13: (288)/(300:312:324)

Round 23: (336)/(350:364:378)

Round 29: (384)/(400:416:432)

Now the colourwork is complete, you have 304:320/(352:368:384)/(400:416:432) sts on your needles.

Using the 3.75mm (UK 9, US 5) needles, knit 1 round, placing two markers, which will denote the arms, as follows: k152:160/(176:184:192)/(200:208:216) sts, PM, k94:100/(108:116:120)/(128:136:142) sts, PM, knit to end of round.

German short rows (GSR)

1. Knit to 5 sts after marker 1, turn work so WS is facing and work a GSR (see Further information, page 136).

2. Purl to 5 sts after marker 2, turn work so RS is facing, bring yarn to front and work a GSR.

3. Knit to 5 sts before preceding GSR, turn work so WS is facing and work a GSR.

4. Purl to 5 sts before preceding GSR, turn work so RS is facing, bring yarn to front and work a GSR.

5. Knit to 5 sts before preceding GSR, turn work so WS is facing and work a GSR.

6. Purl to 5 sts before preceding GSR, turn work so RS is facing, bring yarn to front and work a GSR.

7. Knit to 5 sts before preceding GSR, turn work so WS is facing and work a GSR.

8. Purl to 5 sts before preceding GSR, turn work so RS is facing, bring yarn to front and work a GSR.

9. Knit to start-of-round marker.

10. Knit 1 additional round, working the double-stranded sts (those formed by the GSRs) as a single stitch and removing marker 1 and marker 2.

Knit 0:0/(2:5:5)/(7:8:8) round(s).

Separating the sleeves and the body

Divide for sleeves: k94:100/(108:116:120)/(128:136:142) sts for the back, hold 58:60/(68:68:72)/(72:72:74) sts for the sleeve, cast on 8:10/(10:10:12)/(12:12:12) sts under the armhole, k94:100/(108:116:120)/(128:136:142) sts for the front, hold 58:60/(68:68:72)/(72:72:74) sts for the sleeve, cast on 8:10/(10:10:12)/(12:12:12) sts under the armhole.

Body

You now have 204:220/(236:252:264)/(280:296:308) sts on your needles. Continue to knit until body measures 33:34/(34:35:35)/(35:37:37)cm [13:13½/(13½:13¾:13¾)/(13¾:14½:14½)in] from under armhole, or 5cm (2in) less than desired length.

Swap to 3.5mm (UK 9/10, US 4) needles and work 5cm (2in) in 2×2 rib. Cast off loosely.

Sleeves

Using 3.75mm (UK 9, US 5) needles, take up the suspended sleeve sts and place the 58:60/(68:68:72)/(72:72:74) sts of the sleeve on your needles.

PM to denote the beginning of the round and, starting from the middle of the armhole, pick up 4:5/(5:5:6)/(6:6:6) sts from the centre towards the edge (from right to left). Knit the 58:60/(68:68:72)/(72:72:74) sts of the sleeve then pick up 4:5/(5:5:6)/(6:6:6) sts from the armhole.

You now have 66:70/(78:78:84)/(84:84:86) sts on your needles.

Decrease round: k1, k2tog, knit to third stitch from end of round, ssk, k1 (= 2 decreases).

Rep this decrease round 10:10/(12:12:13)/(13:11:12) more times, every 2.5:2.5/(2:2:2)/(2:2.5:2)cm [1:1/(¾:¾:¾)/(¾:1:¾)in].

Trick

When you pick up the stitches under the arms, a hole can form between the held stitches and the stitches picked up from either side of the armhole. There are a couple of methods of resolving this problem:

+ you can sew up the hole using the ends of the yarn at the end of the project;

+ or you can pick up 2 or 4 additional stitches and work the decrease round until you get down to the number of stitches given in the pattern (see 'Decrease round', above). I recommend this method.

You now have 44:48/(52:52:56)/(56:60:60) sts on your needles.

Continue in st st until the sleeve measures 32cm (12½in), or 10cm (4in) less than the required length: the total length of the sleeve in the pattern is 42cm (16½in).

Swap to 3.5mm (UK 9/10, US 4 needles) and work 10cm (4in) in 2×2 rib. Cast off your sts. Rep for the second sleeve.

Finishing

Weave in ends with a tapestry needle. Block the sweater to smooth out the colourwork and adjust it to the final dimensions.

Scafell final measurements

Note that the measurements given are approximate and very much depend on the swatch.

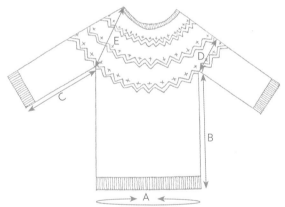

SIZE (cm)	A Around chest	B Body length from bottom of armhole	C Sleeve length from bottom of armhole	D Sleeve width	E Depth of yoke (ribbing included)
85	85cm (33½in)	38cm (15in)	42cm (16½in)	27.5cm (10¾in)	22cm (8¾in)
92	92cm (36¼in)	39cm (15½in)	42cm (16½in)	29cm (11½in)	22cm (8¾in)
98	98.5cm (38¾in)	39cm (15½in)	42cm (16½in)	32.5cm (12¾in)	22.5cm (8¾in)
105	105cm (41¼in)	40cm (16in)	42cm (16½in)	32.5cm (12¾in)	24cm (9½in)
110	110cm (43¼in)	40cm (16in)	42cm (16½in)	35cm (13¾in)	25cm (9¾in)
116	117cm (46in)	40cm (16in)	42cm (16½in)	35cm (13¾in)	26.2cm (10½in)
123	123.3cm (48½in)	42cm (16½in)	42cm (16½in)	35.5cm (14in)	27.5cm (10¾in)
129	128.5cm (50¾in)	42cm (16½in)	42cm (16½in)	36cm (14¼in)	27.5cm (10¾in)

Charts for Scafell sweater and cardigan

☐ MC (main colour)   I Increase

▨ CC1 (contrasting colour 1)   ▨ No stitch

▨ CC2 (contrasting colour 2)

Sizes 85–105cm (33½–41¼in)

Sizes 110–129cm (43¼–50¾in)

Scafell cardigan

The Scafell cardigan is a variation of the sweater of the same name. It is knitted from the neck down in the round then cut down the front to make it into a cardigan using the steek technique. Like the sweater, it has a large circular, colourwork yoke, a straight body and long ribbing at the cuffs and at the bottom of the body. It is finished with a 2×2 rib stitch button band.

YOU WILL NEED

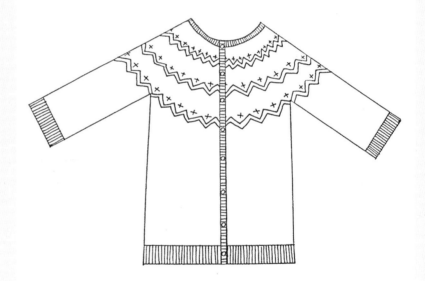

+ **5-ply (sport) yarn**
  · Main colour (MC): 900:
  1,000/(1,100:1,200:1,300)/
  (1,400:1,450:1,500)m [984:
  1,094/(1,203:1,1312:1,1422)/
  (1,531:1,586:1,640)yd]

  · Contrasting colours 1 and 2
  (CC1 and CC2): 150m (164yd)
  for each contrasting colour

+ 3.5mm (UK 9/10, US 4) circular
  needles, for the ribbing, cable
  80cm (31½in)

+ 3.75mm (UK 9, US 5) circular
  needles, for the body
  and sleeves, cable 80cm
  (31½in)

+ 4mm (UK 8, US 6) circular
  needles, for the colourwork
  (optional: only if your tension/
  gauge is a lot tighter when
  you are knitting colourwork),
  cable 80cm (31½in)

+ Stitch markers

+ Waste yarn for stitch holders

+ Tapestry needle

SIZES

85:92/(98:105:110)/(116:123:129)cm [33½:36¼/
(38½:41¼:43¼)/(45½:48½:50¾)in] around the bust
(finished garment measurements)
0 to 10cm (4in) of positive ease recommended

SWATCH 10 × 10CM (4 × 4IN)

24 stitches × 34 rows stocking (stockinette) stitch in the
round using 3.75mm (UK 9, US 5) needles (or another size
depending on your swatch)

Yarns used: Ulysse by De Rerum
Natura, colours Baleine bleue, Quartz
and Ciel (size 85 cm/33½in knitted
with 5cm [2in] positive ease).

Instructions

Yoke

Using 3.5mm (UK 9/10, US 4) needles and the main colour (MC), cast on 97:105/ (113:117:125)/(129:133:133) sts, using the long-tail cast-on method. Join the sts in the round and PM to denote beg of round (which will be at front centre).

Foundation round: k3, PM (S1), continue in 2×2 rib until 2 sts before end, PM (S2), k2.

The 5 sts between the two markers are the **steek sts.** They will be **knitted throughout.** Your round starts at the third st of the steek, namely the central stitch.

Work 4 rounds in 2×2 rib without forgetting to knit the sts between the 2 markers (S1 and S2).

Swap to 3.75mm (UK 9, US 5) needles and knit 1 round.

Knit 1 additional row, increasing 3:0/(2:3:0)/ (1:2:7) sts distributed equally across the round (I recommend using M1L, see Further information, page 136).

You now have 95:100/(110:115:120)/ (125:130:135) sts on your needles and 5 additional sts between the two markers.

Note: these 5 sts (steek) **will not be counted** in the next stitch pattern counts.

Knit 0:0/(1:2:2)/(4:4:4) round(s).

Follow the colourwork chart for your size (see page 129), either continuing with 3.75mm (UK 9, US 5) needles or swapping to 4mm (UK 8, US 6) needles (only if you knit colourwork with a tighter tension/gauge): rep the 16 sts of the chart along the round. You should have 19:20/(22:23:24)/(25:26:27) repetitions of the motif per round.

Note: the first 3 sts of the round and the last 2 are the steek sts. They do not, therefore, have the colourwork motif, but are worked in such a way that you always carry across your contrasting yarns to anchor them as close as possible to the start of the round (in the centre of the steek) so as to reduce the length of the non-knitted strands on the WS of the work.

NOTE

When you work an increase in the chart in the form of M1L or M1R (see Further information, page 136), always pick up the yarn of the MC to work the increase and not that of the CC, then knit the new st with this same colour.

This means that when the steek is cut, all yarns, including even the contrasting ones, will be included inside it.

Here is the stitch count for each round of increases on the chart:

Sizes 85–105cm (33½–41¼in)

Round 2: 152:160/(176:184)

Round 6: 190:200/(220:230)

Round 9: 228:240/(264:276)

Round 19: 266:280/(308:322)

Round 25: 304:320/(352:368)

Sizes 110–129cm (43¼–50¾in)

Round 3: (192)/(200:208:216)

Round 8: (240)/(250:260:270)

Round 13: (288)/(300:312:324)

Round 23: (336)/(350:364:378)

Round 29: (384)/(400:416:432)

Now the colourwork is complete, you have 304:320 / (352:368:384) / (400:416:432) sts on your needles.

Using the 3.75mm (UK 9, US 5) needles, knit 1 round, placing two further markers, which will denote the arms, as follows: k47:50 / (54:58:60) / (64:68:71) sts after (S1), PM, k210:220 / (244:252:264) / (272:280:290), PM. Knit to end of round.

Reminder: markers (S1) and (S2) are the markers that denote the steek while markers 1 and 2 are the markers that indicate where the German short rows should be made at the level of the sleeves.

German short rows (GSR)

1. Knit to 5 sts after marker 2, turn work so WS is facing and work a GSR (see Further information, page 136).

2. Purl to 5 sts after marker 1, turn work so RS is facing, bring yarn to front and work a GSR.

3. Knit to 5 sts before preceding GSR, turn work so WS is facing and work a GSR.

4. Purl to 5 sts before preceding GSR, turn work so RS is facing, bring yarn to front and work a GSR.

5. Knit to 5 sts before preceding GSR, turn work so WS is facing and work a GSR.

6. Purl to 5 sts before preceding GSR, turn work so RS is facing, bring yarn to front and work a GSR.

7. Knit to 5 sts before preceding GSR, turn work so WS is facing and work a GSR.

8. Purl to 5 sts before preceding GSR, turn work so RS is facing, bring yarn to front and work a GSR.

9. Knit to start-of-round marker, working the double-stranded sts (formed by the GSRs) as a single stitch and removing markers 1 and 2.

10. Knit 1 additional round, working the double-stranded sts (those formed by the GSRs) as a single stitch.

Knit 0:0 / (2:5:5) / (7:8:8) rounds.

Separating the sleeves and the body

Divide for sleeves:
k47:50 / (54:58:60) / (64:68:71) sts after marker (S1) for the front, hold 58:60 / (68:68:72) / (72:72:74) sts for the sleeve, cast on 8:10 / (10:10:12) / (12:12:12) sts under the armhole, k94:100 / (108:116:120) / (128:136:142) sts for the back, hold 58:60 / (68:68:72) / (72:72:74) sts for the sleeve, cast on 8:10 / (10:10:12) / (12:12:12) sts under the armhole, knit to end of round.

Body

You now have 204:220 / (236:252:264) / (280:296:308) sts on your needles for the body (the 5 sts of the steek are not counted).

Continue to knit until body measures 33:34 / (34:35:35) / (35:37:37)cm [13:13½ / (13½:13¾:13¾) / (13¾:14½:14½)in] under armhole, or 5cm (2in) less than desired length.

Swap to 3.5mm (UK 9/10, US 4) needles and work 5cm (2in) of 2×2 rib as follows: k3, SM (slip marker), continue in 2×2 rib until 2 sts before end, SM, k2. As for the yoke, the 5 sts of the steek are knitted. Cast off loosely (see Further information, page 137).

Trick

When you pick up the stitches under the arms, a hole can form between the suspended stitches and the stitches picked up from either side of the armhole. There are a couple of methods of resolving this problem:

+ you can sew up the hole using the ends of the yarn at the end of the project;

+ or you can pick up 2 or 4 additional stitches and work the decrease round until you get down to the number of stitches given in the pattern (see 'Decrease round'). I recommend this method.

Sleeves

Using the 3.75mm (UK 9, US 5) needles, place the 58:60/(68:68:72)/(72:72:74) sts of the sleeve on your needles. PM to denote beg of the row and, starting from the middle of the armhole, pick up 4:5/(5:5:6)/(6:6:6) sts from the centre towards the edge (from right to left). Knit the 58:60/(68:68:72)/(72:72:74) sts of the sleeve then pick up 4:5/(5:5:6)/(6:6:6) sts from the armhole.

You now have 66:70/(78:78:84)/(84:84:86) sts on your needles

Decrease round: k1, k2tog, knit to third stitch from end of round, ssk, k1 (= 2 decreases).

Rep this round of decreases 10:10 / (12:12:13) / (13:11:12) more times, every 2.5:2.5/ (2:2:2)/(2:2.5:2)cm [1:1/(¾:¾:¾)/(¾:1:¾)in].

You now have 44:48/(52:52:56)/(56:60:60) sts on your needles.

Continue in st st until the sleeve measures 32cm (12½in), or 10cm (4in) less than the required length: the total length of the sleeve in the pattern is 42cm (16½in).

Swap to 3.5mm (UK 9/10, US 4 needles) and work 10cm (4in) in 2×2 rib. Cast off your sts. Rep for the second sleeve.

Steek

Fasten off the sts either using the crochet method or the sewing machine method (see page 89).

Warning: If you opt for the crochet method, you must first sew a line of sts vertically over the colourwork on the sewing machine. This pattern uses three colours on the same round and the crochet method can only secure two yarns at a time.

Secure the sts first using your chosen method between the LH half of stitch 3 and the RH half of stitch 2, then do the same thing on the other side, using the RH half of stitch 3 and the LH half of stitch 4.

With small, sharp scissors, cut the centre of stitch 3.

Button bands

For the RH side, pick up the sts along the first column of steek stitches, just after the marker: pick up approximately every 2 out of 3 sts, resulting in a number that is a multiple of 4 so you can work a 2×2 rib. Work 2 rows in 2×2 rib.

Row 3 (WS): place markers on certain sts to mark the position of your buttonholes. Start by placing the first one and last one approximately 2 to 3 sts from the top and bottom, then the centre ones at regular intervals.

To form a buttonhole: 2 sts before marked st, p2tog, yo; rep at each marker. You should have around six or seven buttonholes depending on your size.

Work in 2×2 rib across 5 rows and cast off the sts on the next row (working on WS), casting off in rib pattern.

For the LH side, with RS of work facing, pick up the sts along the last column of steek stitches, just before the marker, picking up

the same number of sts as for the RH edge. Work in 2×2 rib across 8 rows, then cast off the sts, casting off in rib pattern on row 9 (working on WS).

Finishing

Weave in ends with a tapestry needle. Block the cardigan to smooth out the colourwork and adjust it to the final dimensions. Sew on the buttons

Scafell final measurements

Note that the measurements given are approximate and very much depend on the swatch.

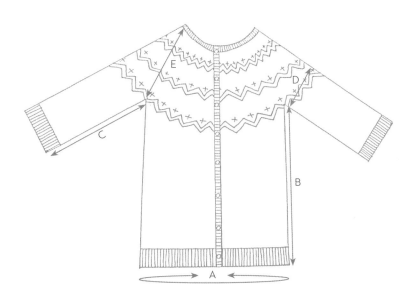

SIZE (cm)	A Around chest	B Body length from bottom of armhole	C Sleeve length from bottom of armhole	D Sleeve width	E Depth of yoke (ribbing included)
85	85cm (33½in)	38cm (15in)	42cm (16½in)	27.5cm (10¾in)	22cm (8¾in)
92	92cm (36¼in)	39cm (15½in)	42cm (16½in)	29cm (11½in)	22cm (8¾in)
98	98.5cm (38¾in)	39cm (15½in)	42cm (16½in)	32.5cm (12¾in)	22.5cm (8¾in)
105	105cm (41¼in)	40cm (16in)	42cm (16½in)	32.5cm (12¾in)	24cm (9½in)
110	110cm (43¼in)	40cm (16in)	42cm (16½in)	35cm (13¾in)	25cm (9¾in)
116	117cm (46in)	40cm (16in)	42cm (16½in)	35cm (13¾in)	26cm (10¼in)
123	123.5cm (48½in)	42cm (16½in)	42cm (16½in)	35.5cm (14in)	27.5cm (10¾in)
129	128.5cm (50¾in)	42cm (16½in)	42cm (16½in)	36cm (14¼in)	27.5cm (10¾in)

Further information

STITCHES USED IN THE PATTERNS

Ribbing in the round

1×1 rib

Row 1: *k1, p1*, rep from * to * to end of row.

Repeat this row across the number of centimetres (inches) given in the pattern.

2×2 rib

Row 1: *k2, p2*, rep from * to * to end of row.

Repeat this row across the number of centimetres (inches) given in the pattern.

Increases

M1R: make one right, an increase where the stitch leans towards the right.

Using the point of the left needle, pick up the horizontal bar between the stitches from back to front. Knit this stitch, slipping the right needle through the front leg to create a twist.

M1L: make one left, an increase where the stitch leans towards the left.

Using the point of the left needle, pick up the horizontal bar between the stitches from front to back. Knit this stitch through the back leg.

Decreases

K2tog: knit two stitches together.

Ssk: slip two stitches one after the other knitwise (slipping them from the left needle to the right needle), then knit them together on the right needle.

German short rows

Short rows allow you to knit more rows on one side of the knit than the other. For a certain number of rows, you will no longer knit in the round, but turn your piece and work in rows.

These rows must be worked in a particular way so as not to create holes.

In the projects in the book, they are used to knit more rows on the back than on the front, which will deepen the neckline and make the garment more comfortable to wear.

German short rows are worked in two stages: first on the right side, then on the wrong side.

Knit until you reach the stitch stated in the pattern, then turn the work. With the yarn in front, slip the first stitch on the left needle purlwise to the right needle. Pull the yarn gently towards the back, until two stitches form and bring the yarn back to the front.

Purl across the row until you reach the stitch stated in the pattern, then turn the work. Bring the yarn to the front, slip the first stitch on the left needle on to the right needle, purlwise. Pull the yarn gently towards the back, until two stitches form. Knit row.

Stretchy cast-offs
For stretchy cast-offs, cast off the stitches loosely using a larger needle size.

There are also other techniques – you can easily find video tutorials online (for example, search for Elizabeth Zimmermann's sewn bind-off technique, Jeny's Surprisingly Stretchy Bind Off or tubular cast off/bind off).

Anna Dervout - Along avec Anna

My love affair with all things handmade goes back to my childhood. I spent hours in my grandma's attic (the 'sewing room') with my cousins, rummaging through the piles of pillous (a Breton word for fabrics) or the assortment of offcuts provided by my mother. So many happy times were spent sewing by hand or on the machine, nurturing a passion that is still with me today.

Knitting came much later, when I was pregnant with my daughter in 2015. In my youth I had made a few attempts at knitting woolly scarves on straight needles, but had never really got the hang of it. It was only when I was pregnant, surrounded by my friends in Montreal, all of whom are greater sewers and knitters, that I started to get the bug. They introduced me to 'modern' knitting, to the beautiful patterns available on Ravelry that are knitted in the round, to beautiful hand-dyed yarns... and a passion was born. This passion has a huge place in my life and I have rarely been without needles since.

My blog Along avec Anna was launched in December 2013 to share my sewing projects and it became a sewing and knitting blog in 2015. Not long afterwards, I began a podcast on YouTube. In my blog, I share my sewing and knitting projects as well as giving tutorials. My patterns are available to buy on the Ravelry site.

Creating patterns came as a matter of course; after two years of quite intense knitting. I had ideas for things I wanted to do, and felt the need to get them down on paper. The Dandelion cardigan came out in August 2017 and was so well received that I decided to continue. My passion became my livelihood – I could not have wished for anything better.

I have been lucky enough to be followed by a community of enthusiasts who have supported me in the various projects I undertake, and it is thanks to them that I have been able to write this book for you today.

Online:

Blog: www.alongavecanna.com
Instagram: @along.avec.anna
Facebook: @alongavecanna
YouTube: Along avec Anna
Ravelry: Anna Dervout
Patreon: Along avec Anna

Acknowledgements

Thank you to Aude, my editor, for believing in this project and for putting her trust in me. Thanks for her advice and kindness. Thanks to Armelle and Sophie for their proofreading.

Thanks to Solenn from De Rerum Natura, Pauline and Tristan from Lain'amourée and Christine from trÍScote for agreeing to be partners in this project and for believing in me enough to allow me to put their yarns on display.

Thank you to my friends in Montreal: Audrey, Amélie, Mélina, Ariane and Perrine, who gave me this passion for knitting and taught me so much. I owe you a lot!

Thank you to my Patreon subscribers for helping me in this project by giving me your opinion or testing out the patterns. Thank you for your investment! A special thanks to Maude and Amélie who helped me knit the children's versions of the projects in this book, and to Pauline and Delphine for lending me their versions of Bowfell and Helvellyn for the photos.

Thanks to my family – especially my mum – for their day-to-day support. Thanks to Anne H. for advising me at the beginning of this project. Thanks to my friends Elise D. (my Belgian friend), Sandra, Elise D. (my friend from Nantes) and Caroline, for their proofreading and support. Thank you to Lise for her many pieces of advice and our valuable discussions. And a huge thank you to my cousin Klaire for the technical diagrams and help with some of the photos; she is always there to help me when I need it!

Thanks to you, Harry, for your dedication since the beginning of my blog, for your beautiful pictures of the patterns and for all that you bring to me every day. Thank you to my little Alice, who inspires me on a daily basis and agrees (more or less) to act as a model for my patterns.

Finally, thank you to all the people who follow me on my blog, Patreon, Instagram, Ravelry or on YouTube, and who encourage me and support me in my different projects. It is thanks to you that I have had the opportunity to write this book.

Partners

DE RERUM NATURA

'Because I dreamt of good quality, beautiful wool between my fingers and on my children's backs; because I really wanted to believe that we didn't have to close our eyes to our wool's unknown origins, disastrous carbon footprint and dubious breeding conditions to savour the pleasure of an attractive yarn that slides over our needles; because I met breeders and industrialists who showed initiative when it came to imagining other possibilities; because I sincerely believe that doing things with our hands, our hearts and our minds can help us shape a more beautiful world.'

De Rerum Natura is a French brand that has been producing knitting yarns designed to highlight local resources and knowledge since 2013. All the yarns are made in France and Italy (for those stages of the process that can no longer be carried out in France) from natural raw materials (organic Arles merino, black merino from Portugal, organic linen and silk).

These yarns are organic and ethical as well as soft and beautiful to knit and wear. They have set a new bar in terms of local wool and are a stepping stone to a future where there will be sheep in the mountains, small flourishing spinning mills and all sorts of happy knitters...

De Rerum Natura yarns can be ordered directly on the brand's website or are available to buy in a few bricks and mortar outlets such as YAK in Brighton and Lanaé Tricot in Grenoble.

De Rerum Natura: http://dererumnatura.fr

YAK, 16 Gloucester Rd, Brighton BN1 4AD, UK
yarnandknitting.com

Boutique Lanaé Tricot, 5, rue Genissieu, 38000 Grenoble, France: www.lanae-tricot.com

LAIN'AMOURÉE

'Softness in colour'

Lain'amourée is a brand of hand-dyed wool. The yarns are all lovingly dyed by Pauline and Tristan in the Loire Valley, France.

Softness and delicacy are their watchwords. The colours progress across a pastel palette, using noble, luxurious materials ranging from merino to silk or baby alpaca, and including rarer wools such as yak and baby camel.

Each colour tells a story so, stitch by stitch, you can knit up your dreams with your needles and enjoy a few rows of escapism.

Pauline and Tristan's yarns are available directly from the brand's website, but are also sold in the bricks and mortar shop listed below, in London.

Lain'amourée: lainamouree.com

Beautiful Knitters, 53 Moreton Street, Pimlico, London SW1V 2NY, UK: beautifulknitters.co.uk

 # trÍScote

TRÍSCOTE

Christine, the founder of trÍScote, first visited Iceland in 2004. She had always been a knitter, and was immediately enchanted by the colours of Icelandic wool, the colourwork patterns and the seamless knitted jumpers.

A few years later, in 2011, her passion for Iceland and Icelandic knitting grew into trÍScote. The range she sells has since expanded to include Icelandic Lopi wool and the Danish brand Filcolana, as well as other favourite products, knitting materials and pattern ideas.

In addition to the online shop **www.triscote.fr**, trÍScote is involved in promoting Icelandic knitting through knitting workshops at Iceland-related events.

trÍScote yarns are available through UK retailers such as No Frills Knitting:

No Frills Knitting, 15 Cannon Street, Bedminster, Bristol BS3 1BH, UK
www.nofrillsknitting.co.uk

First published in Great Britain 2024 by
Search Press Limited
Wellwood, North Farm Road,
Tunbridge Wells, Kent TN2 3DR

Original French title: *Tricoter le jacquard en rond*
© 2021 Éditions Eyrolles, Paris, France

English translation by Burravoe Translation Services

Illustrations (technical diagrams): Klaire Jamsworth
Photographs: Anna Dervout
Graphic design and layout: Julie Simoens

ISBN: 978-1-80092-121-4
ebook ISBN: 978-1-80093-110-7

Suppliers
If you have difficulty in obtaining any of the materials and equipment mentioned in this book, then please visit the Search Press website for details of suppliers:
www.searchpress.com

Bookmarked Hub
For further ideas and inspiration, and to join our free online community,
visit www.bookmarkedhub.com

The projects in this book have been made using metric measurements, and the imperial equivalents provided have been calculated following standard conversion practices. The imperial measurements are often rounded to the nearest ⅛in for ease of use except in rare circumstances; however, if you need more exact measurements, there are a number of excellent online converters that you can use. Always use either metric or imperial measurements, not a combination of both.